Student Workbook
for
Communication Voices

Amy M. Smith

Sarah E. Symonds

Myra M. Shird

North Carolina Agricultural
& Technical University

KENDALL/HUNT PUBLISHING COMPANY
4050 Westmark Drive   Dubuque, Iowa 52002

Dedication

Both of the authors would like to acknowledge Joyce Ferguson for providing the first step in what has been a roller coaster journey; without her this book would not be possible. Thanks also go to their students from North Carolina A&T for suggestions and growth, friends and colleagues from University of North Carolina Greensboro, and Dr. Myra Shird for providing this opportunity.

My heartfelt thanks go to my friends and family for all the support, love, and encouragement you have given me throughout this process. I appreciate everything you have done for me. I also want to express my gratitude to Deborah Burris for offering me her guidance, wisdom, and friendship.

Amy M. Smith

I would like to take this opportunity to thank my friends and family for their love and support; my new colleagues at Coastal Carolina for their support and suggestions; and my co-author, Amy Smith, for her suggestion in doing this book and dedication to seeing it completed.

Sarah E. Symonds

Contents

Introduction

Dear Student,

In this workbook you will find activities that correlate not only to your class readings, but also to your everyday life. The first half of this workbook features activities that will help you understand yourself, your communication style, and your relationships with others better. The second half of this workbook is designed to enhance your organization skills. You will notice how the outlines might appear "incomplete." We thought about this and know that as students, you will need to know how to organize your thoughts. The outlines are designed this way so that you can practice organizing.

We feel that communication is the basis for all human interaction, and is well worth the time and effort you need to expend to master it. We hope that you will enjoy the outlines, activities, and self-tests in this workbook. Use them to excel in your coursework, as well as to enhance your communication skills, both with yourself and with others.

Sincerely,

Amy M. Smith
Sarah E. Symonds

chapter one

Introduction to Human Communication

Chapter Outline

I. Telling Stories as a Way of Knowing

    A. Standpoint Theory

        1. Georg Wilhelm Hegel (1807) introduced the concept of Standpoint Theory in his discussion of the different standpoints or viewpoints present in the master-slave relationship.

        2. Hegel shows that while both slave and master exist in the same society, their viewpoints on that society are extremely different.

        3. The ultimate conclusion is that there is no single viewpoint of social life.

        4. Our viewpoints are influenced by our position in life.

    B. Narrative research is necessary to obtain multiple viewpoints of communication.

        1. Casey says that narrative research is, "at present, distinctly, interdisciplinary, including elements of literary, historical, anthropological, sociological, psychological, and cultural studies."

        2. Riessman adds, "A primary way individuals make sense of experience is by casting it in narrative form."

II. Communicating by Definition

    A. Communication is a systematic process in which we share ideas and create meaning through human symbolic action.

        1. Communication is systematic in that there are interrelated parts that affect one another.

        2. Communication is a process because it is ongoing.

            a. You cannot **NOT** communicate.

            b. The meaning of our communication relies heavily on the "other's" interpretations of our symbolic actions.

            c. Symbolic action refers to our usage of verbal, as well as nonverbal symbols to create meaning.

            d. The concept of shared meaning arises out of our agreement on the meaning of the symbols.

        3. Symbols-verbal and nonverbal-are actually ambiguous, arbitrary, and abstract representations.

    B. Speech communication is a humanistic and scientific discipline that focuses on how, why, and what effect communication has on people.

III. Communication-"How You Do Dat Dere"? The Communication Model.
   A. The sender is the source of the message.
   B. The receiver is the interpreter of the message.
   C. Motivation arises out of the personal benefit we receive from putting our thoughts and feelings out there for public scrutiny.
   D. Encoding is the process of putting our messages into a form that can be communicated.
   E. Decoding is the process that the receiver goes through in order to interpret the sender's message.
   F. We transport our messages using three different types of codes.
      1. Verbal codes (language) are the means of transporting our messages using the spoken word.
      2. Vocal codes (paralanguage) are the vocal elements that accompany the spoken word. These codes include the volume, pitch, rate, and inflections of the voice.
      3. Visual codes (nonverbal) are behaviors that we use to communicate messages, such as facial expressions, gestures, posture, appearance, etc.
   G. Feedback is the receiver's response to the sender's message.
      1. It can be intentional, which verbal responses generally are.
      2. Feedback can be unintentional, which is sometimes the case with nonverbal feedback.
   H. Noise interrupts or interferes with the intended message. Noise impacts how we receive the message. Noise stems from external as well as internal factors.
      1. External factors are those things that exist in our environment.
      2. Internal noise arises on the inside of us.
   I. Channels of communication are simply the vehicles that transmit messages from sender to receiver.
IV. You Hear Me, but Are You Listening?
   A. Hearing is the physiological process that takes place when sound waves hit the tympanic membrane and are transmitted to the site of sensory reception.
   B. Listening is a cognitive process with six very distinct steps: being mindful, hearing, selecting, interpreting, responding, and remembering.
      1. Being mindful is the first step. Mindfulness is being present in the moment, being focused on what is going on here and now.
      2. Hearing, the second part of the process, is the physical reception of the message. Hearing takes place when sound waves hit the eardrum.
      3. We select to entertain or pay attention to certain communication and disregard other communication. We are interested in those things that speak directly to our personal motivations. Once we have selected communication to focus on, we organize that communication based on our own personal "mental" categories.
      4. We apply meaning by interpreting the message.
      5. Responding to the message is a crucial step in the listening process. Responding allows for clarification; it reinforces the crux of the message.
      6. The final step in the listening process is remembering. Essentially, we forget approximately two-thirds of what we ever hear.

C. Why don't we listen more critically?
1. We don't listen because we are absorbed in our own thoughts and concerns.
2. We hold prejudices and prejudge others and their communication.
3. We do not put forth the effort.
4. We fake listening.
5. We divert the conversation from the person who is speaking so that the conversation focuses on us.
6. We only focus on a particular piece or part that is being communicated to us.
7. We listen only so that canwe can ambush the speaker.

V. Where Do We Go from Here?
A. The study of communication goes back more than 2,000 years.
B. There are several different fields in communication.
1. Intrapersonal communication is communication with oneself.
2. Interpersonal communication deals with communication between people.
3. Small group communication allows us to understand how people solve problems, make decisions, and work in the group context.
4. Organizational communication focuses on how we communicate in organizations and corporate entities.
5. Cultural communication is the study of how our values, beliefs, and way of life impact our communication.
6. Public communication or public speaking is presentations or giving speeches.

Name: _____ *Section:* _____*Date:* _____

1.1 Your Narrative

The Standpoint Theory, introduced by Wilhelm Hegel, proposes that there is not one single viewpoint of social life. Everyone's life is filled with narratives. In the space provided, write your narrative, or story, centering around how you got to college.

_____

_____

_____

_____

_____

_____

_____

_____

_____

_____

After writing your story, compare your narrative with a classmate. Note how your stories differ. How do the differences relate to your standpoints?

_____

_____

_____

_____

_____

_____

_____

1.2 Somebody Else's Story

Read Marissa Dick's story, as provided in your textbook. Next, imagine that you have the opportunity to interview and introduce your hero to an audience. In the space provided, write the questions that you would ask your hero in order to get their story. After writing the questions, brainstorm an introduction that you would like to use to introduce your hero.

Questions

Introduction

_____

_____

_____

_____

_____

_____

Name: _____   *Section:* _____ *Date:* _____

1.3 Create a Communication Model

Using the Transactional Model in Chapter 1, diagram a recent conversation you participated in. Be as creative as possible when creating your diagram. Make sure you use pieces of the actual conversation to show understanding of sender, receiver, encoding, decoding, channels, noise, and context.

1.4 Being Mindful[1]

Part A

The first step of the listening process is being mindful. While on the phone with a friend, turn on the television or the radio. After you get off the phone, write down what you remember about the conversation. Next, while on the phone with the same friend, be completely in the moment, with no distractions. When the conversation is finished, write down what you remember about the conversation.

_____

_____

_____

_____

_____

_____

_____

Part B–Analysis

What did you notice about your listening behaviors? How hard was it to be mindful of what your friend was saying? What differences did you note between the conversations? Were there any similarities? What conclusions can you draw about being in the moment?

_____

_____

_____

_____

_____

_____

_____

[1]Adapted from L.E. Assante. *Student workbook: Communication for Verderbers* 10th Edition. (Belmont, CA: Wadsworth Publishing, 2002), 94.

Name: _____ *Section:* _____ *Date:* _____

1.5 Every Good Boy Deserves Fudge

One device that helps individuals remember what they listened to is to create a mnemonic. Mnemonics are useful memory devices. Using the space provided, create a mnemonic for the six phases of the listening process, as described in Chapter 1 of your textbook.

1.6 Critical Listening in Popular Culture

Select a song off a CD or the radio. Using the critical listening skills in chapter one, write a summary of the message the song is conveying. How do the lyrics coincide or contradict with the music. What format would this song be played on if it were on the radio? Who is the target audience for that type of radio station? Is the song (lyrics and music) appropriate for the intended audience?

_____

_____

_____

_____

_____

_____

_____

_____

_____

_____

_____

_____

_____

_____

_____

_____

_____

_____

Name: _____ *Section:* _____*Date:* _____

1.7 Examples of Communication

Define and offer examples of each type of communication discussed in Chapter 1:

Intrapersonal Communication: _____

_____

_____

Interpersonal Communication: _____

_____

_____

Small Group Communication: _____

_____

_____

Organizational Communication: _____

_____

_____

Cultural Communication: _____

_____

_____

Public Communication: _____

_____

_____

1.8 Prioritizing Your Standpoint

Using the story from Activity 1.1, make a list of the characteristics that make up your standpoint. Once you have compiled your list, rewrite the list in order of the importance you place on each characteristic.

Name: _____ Section: _____ Date: _____

Test Yourself

Match these vocabulary terms with the descriptions that best define them.

1. _____ Hearing   a. Communication between people

2. _____ Selecting   b. Forming messages to be communicated

3. _____ Interpreting   c. Interrupts or interferes with intended messages

4. _____ Frame of Reference   d. Paying attention to certain messages

5. _____ Noise   e. Interpreting the sender's message

6. _____ Channels   f. Our background and personal experiences

7. _____ Encoding   g. Self-talk

8. _____ Decoding   h. Assigning meaning to the message

9. _____ Intrapersonal Communication   i. Physical reception of the message

10. _____ Interpersonal Communication   j. Vehicles that transmit messages

chapter Two

Perception and Social Responsibility

Chapter Outline

I. Perception as Making Sense of the World

    A. Perception is the complex process of selecting, organizing, and interpreting information about people, events, activities, and situations.

        1. We rely on all of our senses to gather information about our surrounding environment.

        2. From the information we gain, we try to make sense of the world around us.

    B. Perception is ultimately about how we select, organize, and interpret information so that we can understand our surroundings.

II. Selection as Meeting Our Needs

    A. We select to focus on information that *meets our physiological and psychological needs.*

    B. We select to focus on information that *interests* us.

    C. We select to focus on *that which we expect to see.*

III. Organizing as a Means of Categorizing

    A. We organize information based on our personal categorizing system.

        1. We categorize based on our personal experiences and based on the material and nonmaterial components of our cultural.

        2. Cognitive psychology suggests that we organize information into *schema* or patterns that are coherent and meaningful.

        3. A variety of schemata helps us to organize our impressions: prototypes, mental yardsticks, and stereotypes.

            a. A prototype is the benchmark for how we categorize a person, object, activity, or situation.

            b. A mental yardstick allows us to measure new information, using the prototype as the primary basis of comparison.

            c. Stereotyping is the categorizing of people, situations, and objects, without acknowledging unique individual characteristics.

        4. How we organize our perceptions is inextricably linked to our past experiences.

            a. Past experiences may cloud or distort perceptions.

            b. It is a social responsibility to make sure that what we see and/or hear represents reality.

IV. Accurate Stereotypes, Do They Exist?

    A. We usually develop stereotypes based on our personal experiences or the experiences of those close to us.

    B. Stereotypes are linked to our frame of reference.

    C. Some generalizations provide understanding and expectations for how people, situations, and objects should be.

        1. Generalizations sometimes provide a basis for us to compare our expectations with reality.

        2. In this society, generalizations or stereotypes frequently inform our behaviors, such as your decision to run.

V. I'm a Product of My Environment

    A. Attribution is the process of understanding the reasons for our own as well as other's behaviors.

        1. We attempt to understand behaviors by attributing cause to either the individual's situation (environment) or the individual's disposition (personality traits).

        2. We must remember that the attributions that we make are not always correct.

    B. We make an attribution error when we overestimate dispositional causes and underestimate situational causes of others' actions.

    C. This self-serving bias distorts our perceptions of our worth in relation to others in the world. We develop an unrealistic image of ourselves and our abilities when we perceive ourselves as invincible, omnipotent, and the alpha and omega of any situation.

VI. Factors That Influence Perception

    A. Physiological, psychological, cultural, and gender factors influence perception. In addition, perception is greatly influenced by the media.

    B. Perceptual Differences Based on Physiology

        1. Physical factors such as age, weight, height, health, and body shape account for perceptual differences.

        2. Other physiological factors may impact perception on multiple levels.

    C. Perceptual Differences Based on State of Mind

        1. State of mind greatly influences perception.

        2. Perceptions are distorted because of their negative state of mind.

    D. Perceptual Differences Based on Culture

        1. Culture is a way of life because it encompasses values, beliefs, and understandings shared by a group of people.

        2. Cultures that are communal value the family over the individual.

        3. Co-cultures are social communities within a macro or dominant culture.

            a. Co-cultures have a system of values and beliefs that may coincide or conflict with those of the dominant culture.

            b. People can belong to multiple co-cultures.

            c. Members of co-cultures have unique understandings of the world.

            d. Our perceptions are influenced by the personal knowledge that comes from our experiences as members of a particular social community.

E. Perceptual Differences Based on Gender
   1. Women tend to perceive need.
      a. Women have been raised to be caring, to take care of the house and the family.
      b. Women are the nurturers in this culture.
   2. Gender roles are socially constructed and greatly influence our understanding of the world.
F. Perception and Media Influence
   1. Media has much influence on perception.
   2. The media defines what the public is to perceive as a crisis, what it is to perceive as a scandal, what it is to perceive as newsworthy, what it is to perceive as trendy, what it is to perceive as hot, and what it is to perceive as not.
VII. Improving Perception Competencies
   A. Be Mindful
   B. Seek More information to Verify Perceptions
   C. Distinguish Facts from Inferences
      1. A fact is a statement that can be demonstrated as true or false, regardless of our own personal beliefs.
      2. An inference involves personal preferences and opinions.
   D. Perform a Perception Audit
      1. A perception audit is the process of examining your perceptions against reality.
      2. It is our social responsibility to evaluate our perceptions of those changed people, situations, and objects.
   E. Be Open to New Ways of Experiencing the World

Name: _____ *Section:* _____ *Date:* _____

2.1 How Quickly They Forget[1]

In this activity, students have the opportunity to see how difficult it is to recall the details of a face they were introduced to just moments before.

Find a person that you are not familiar with. Introduce yourself to that person. After about ten seconds, arrange yourself back-to-back with the person. Explain that they are not to look back at their partners. For about thirty seconds write what you remember about your partner and what your first impression of the individual is.

Next, answer the following questions.

1. Was it easier or harder depending on the gender? _____

   _____

2. What is the first thing you notice? _____

   _____

3. What is the last thing you remembered? _____

   _____

4. Is it easy to recall specific details after a brief meeting? _____

   _____

---

[1]Adapted from E. West, *201 Icebreakers: Group-Mixers, Warm-Ups, Eenergizers, and Playful Activities.* (New York, NY, McGraw-Hill, 1997), 56-57.

2.2 Personal Ads[2]

Write a personal ad in the space below to post in the classroom for your fellow classmates to read. In class, post the advertisements for each person to read and guess
which member of the class wrote the ad. Answer the questions provided.

Personal Ad

_____

_____

_____

_____

_____

_____

_____

Questions

1. As a viewer of the ads, how did you determine to whom the ad belonged since you
   could not base it on race and gender?

2. How important is race and gender in getting to know a person?

3. What did you learn about yourself while writing the ad?

4. What did you learn about others?

5. How did it make you feel to have others viewing your ad?

6. How did your preconceived notions influence your guess for the ads?

---

[2]Adapted from E. West, *201 Icebreakers: Group-Mixers, Warm-Ups, Eenergizers, and Playful Activities.* (New York, NY,
McGraw-Hill, 1997), 155.

Name: _____ *Section:* _____ *Date:* _____

2.3 Experiencing a New Culture

This is a four-part assignment. First, students will write down their preconceived notions of a culture that they have never participated in.

Next, students will participate in a culture, different from their own, by attending a religious service, festival, eating dinner with a family, or some way of *experiencing* the culture. (Some students tutored Montagnards or volunteered at a special needs or an elderly home).

Third, students will conduct an interview. (It is preferred that you do the interview after the first participation because you will have an experience from which to draw questions.)

Finally, students will design a collage of the culture. The collage should reflect your assumptions about the culture prior to the experience, your preconceived notions of the culture, the knowledge that you gained from the experience, and application to a theory of interpersonal communication. This collage should be at 36 by 48. Collages could contain pictures from your experience and your interview as well as pictures from magazines and digital photos.

Ideas from students (different from the norm) include: Native American, Muslim, Jehovah's Witness, and African-American churches, Greeks, Adopt-A-Grandparent Program, Jewish funerals, How to Convert to Judaism, Universalist Church, Gothics, a Country Bar, and Country Club Culture.

Questions

1. How were your preconceived notions different from your actual experience?

2. What influences your preconceived notions?

3. What important lessons did you learn from your experiences?

4. What lessons have you been able to share with others?

2.4 Factors That Influence Perception

Think of a particular event you have witnessed or participated in. List and discuss examples of how each factor influenced your perception on that event.

Physiology: _____

_____

_____

Psychological: _____

_____

_____

Cultural: _____

_____

_____

Gender: _____

_____

_____

Name: _____ Section: _____ Date: _____

2.5 Perception and Media Influence

View a newscast on a major television network. Make a list of the news stories discussed. Keep track of how long or short each news item was discussed and any particular language or graphics that were used to tell each story. Compare the items from the television shows with the items in the next day's newspaper. Which items were given equal coverage (maximum time frame/print space), different coverage, or no coverage from one news outlet or the other?

_____

_____

_____

_____

_____

_____

_____

_____

_____

_____

_____

_____

_____

_____

_____

_____

_____

_____

2.6 Do Accurate Stereotypes Exist?

Make a list of stereotypes that exist for each of the following groups. Discuss why you think the stereotypes originated, their accuracy, and whether they are positive or negative stereotypes.

Caucasians:

African Americans:

Hispanic Americans:

Asian Americans:

Police Officers:

Firefighters:

Musicians:

Actors:

Athletes:

Name: _____ Section: _____ Date: _____

Test Yourself

Match these vocabulary terms with the descriptions that best define them.

1. _____ Selection   a. Benchmark

2. _____ Organizing   b. Mental factors that affect perception

3. _____ Interpreting   c. Personal preference and opinions

4. _____ Prototype   d. Paying attention to certain messages

5. _____ Mental Yardstick   e. Comparison using the benchmark

6. _____ Stereotype   f. Assigning meaning

7. _____ Physiological   g. Values and beliefs that affect perception

8. _____ Psychological   h. Personal categorizing system

9. _____ Cultural   i. Generalization of people, objects, and situations

10. _____ Inference   j. Physical factors that affect perception

Chapter Three

Culture as Worldview: Individualism and Collectivism in Communication

Chapter Outline

I. Culture as Worldview: Individualism and Collectivism in Communication

    A. Definition of Culture

        1. Culture is your thoughts, your beliefs, your attitudes, your values, your behaviors, your look, your clothes, your speech patterns, your language, your notion of gender roles, your valued relationships, your use of time, your management of conflict, your self-disclosure, your acceptance of others' views, and much more.

        2. Culture is your way of life.

    B. Material and Nonmaterial Components of Culture

        1. The concept of co-culture is a way of expressing pieces of our individuality that we have in common with others, but not with the entire populace.

        2. Culture consists of material and nonmaterial components.

            a. Material components of culture are things that rise out of our way of life and that have been physically created by humans.

            b. Nonmaterial components of culture are intangible constructions that impact how we behave and think.

                i. Beliefs are those things that we consider as truth.

                ii. Values are those things that we believe to be good, right, and worthwhile in life.

                iii. Norms are informal rules that govern our social and personal conduct. Norms arise out of tradition, which is communicated to us from generation to generation. Norms characterize that which is appropriate and normal in various situations.

    C. Language molds our perceptions of life, perceptions of ourselves, and our perceptions of ourselves in relation to others in the world.

II. Individualistic and Collectivistic Cultures

    A. Individualistic cultures are those cultures that place greater emphasis on the individual person rather than the group.

B. Collectivistic cultures are those cultures that focus on the collective or group rather than the individual person.

C. The dimensions of individualism and collectivism exist on a continuum.

D. Approach to Knowledge

1. Approach to knowledge refers to how we come to "know" what is real and what is truth.

2. In individualistic cultures the focus is on the objective or tangible.

3. Collectivistic cultures focus on the subjective experience of a thing to "know" it. Knowledge comes from the feelings associated with the thing.

E. Thought/Speech Patterns

1. How we think affects how we speak.

2. Linear thinkers will produce linear or deductive arguments that go from point A to point B.

3. Circular thinkers will produce inductive arguments that go from specific events, examples, or instances to more general points.

   a. Circular thinkers may go from point A to point C to point B to point E and back to point A in making their argument.

   b. Circular speakers can be quite frustrating to linear thinkers because the arguments are "too scattered" for them to follow.

F. Interaction Guiding Principle

1. The principle that guides interaction in communication events is what is valued by that particular culture.

2. Collective cultures value courtesy, harmony and peace; therefore, peace and harmony are sought during interaction by being courteous.

3. Individualistic cultures value candor and honesty more.

G. Time

1. Time functions in different ways in individualistic and collectivistic cultures.

2. In individualistic cultures, time is viewed as monochronic (singular events occurring at one time).

   a. It is valued in its linear form based on the actual time, thus, the emphasis on not wasting time.

   b. This approach to time is one that values scheduling time and keeping to that schedule.

3. In collectivistic cultures time is polychronic (multiple events occurring simultaneously). Time is not controlled by a schedule but rather by relationships.

4. When monochronic and polychronic cultures come together, there is often misunderstanding.

   a. The differential approaches to time can create problems for polychronic people in a monochronic society.

   b. It is crucial that the implications of working on a monochronic schedule be understood.

3.1 It's a Small World After All

Examine five cultural aspects of your life that your family follows. For example, if your family uses an Advent calendar every Christmas, write down what you remember about the tradition. Next, research the tradition. Find out everything you can about that tradition.

_____

_____

_____

_____

_____

_____

_____

_____

Questions

1. Did this tradition originate in your culture? _____

_____

2. What surprised you about this tradition? _____

_____

3. What new things did you learn about this tradition? _____

_____

3.2 A Wide-Wide World

The main idea of this project is to find out things about people that people don't take time usually take time to find out because of their cultural background. This activity allows students to examine a culture completely different from their own. For example, if you are from an individualistic culture, pick an individual from a collectivistic culture.

Go out and find someone of another cultural background and shadow that person long enough to gather unique and genuine information on that particular culture. For example, a person of Caucasian and African-American descent would most likely shadow a Mexican, Chinese, or Arab person.

Fill in the chart below with your observations about the person.

	Individualistic	Collectivistic
Approach to Knowledge		
Thought/Speech Pattern		
Interaction Guiding Principle		
Time		
Masculine/Feminine Culture		

This assignment is for each individual to understand the key components of culture and then to better understand different cultures in the world today by getting hands-on practice.

Name: _____ Section: _____ Date: _____

3.3 Afrocentric Philosophical Foundations

After reading the section titled "Afrocentric Philosophical Foundations" in Chapter 3, think about what African-American traditions you celebrate or are aware of. Then answer the following questions.

1. How do these customs impact your communication with others about your/their heritage?

2. Do you share these customs with family members or friends? If yes, in what ways? If no, why not?

3. Where did you learn these traditions?

4. Why and how are these traditions important to you, as an individual?

5. How do you inform others of these traditions and cultures?

6. Are these customs indicative of an individualistic or a collectivistic culture? Why?

3.4 Topsy-Turvy

Write a brief essay describing the culture that you live in (individualistic or collectivistic). Once you have described the current culture, imagine that your culture was flipped, and you now live in the opposite culture. Elaborate on what that world would look like.

_____

_____

_____

_____

_____

_____

_____

_____

_____

_____

_____

_____

_____

_____

_____

_____

Name: _____ *Section:* _____ *Date:* _____

3.5 Interaction Guiding Principle

Keep a log of your conversations for one day. What does your interaction guiding principle look like? Do you value candor or courtesy more? If you used both, discuss when it is appropriate to use candor instead of courtesy, or vice versa.

3.6 What Time Is It?

Make a list of settings where polychronic and monochronic time are appropriate in your culture. Discuss why it is appropriate to use one over the other in particular situations.

Polychronic	Monochronic

Name: _____ *Section:* _____ *Date:* _____

Test Yourself

Match these vocabulary terms with the descriptions that best define them.

1. _____ Individualistic Cultures   a. Deductive

2. _____ Collectivistic Cultures   b. Singular events occurring at one time

3. _____ Objective   c. Truth

4. _____ Subjective   d. Culture centered on each person

5. _____ Linear   e. Inductive

6. _____ Circular   f. Multiple realities

7. _____ Candor   g. Harmony

8. _____ Courtesy   h. Culture centered on group

9. _____ Monochronic   i. Multiple events occurring simultaneously

10. _____ Polychronic   j. Singular reality

Chapter Four

Communication and the "Self"

Chapter Outline

I. Defining Self

    A. Julia Wood says self, "develops over time and, therefore is a process."

    B. Researchers claim that we are not born with selves, but instead we acquire them.

II. The Self That Is Communicated to Us

    A. Self is the multidimensional product that results from the complex process of internalizing and acting from direct definitions that we receive as we communicate.

    B. Labels that define for us who we are and how we are to behave are direct definitions. Direct definitions communicate to us who our parents and society see us as.

    C. Limitations of Others' Definitions

        1. Self-fulfilling prophecy is when we act in ways that bring about expectations or judgments of ourselves.

        2. Self-sabotage arises out of negative self-talk.

    D. Particular and Generalized Others

        1. Particular others are the people that initially communicate to us who we are and what is expected of us.

            a. Particular others include mother, father, siblings, aunts, uncles, cousins, and day care providers.

            b. Parenting styles communicate to us who we are and how we are to approach others and relationships.

                i. If our parents have been consistently positive in our lives and consistently loving, we will tend to have a higher self-esteem and positive view of others.

                ii. If our parents rejected us and abused us, we are likely to feel bad about ourselves, see others as not loving, and we may fear getting into relationships.

                iii. When parents are disinterested in us, we tend to become disinterested in others.

                iv. When parents are inconsistent with how they treat us, the parenting style yields an individual with low self-esteem.

        2. The generalized other is the faceless group of rules and roles accepted by our social community.

            a. The generalized other represents society's concerted views.

   b. Through communication, we internalize the perspectives of the generalized other and come to accept the perspectives of the generalized others as our own.

   c. The American culture tends to emphasize race, gender, sexual orientation, and socioeconomic class.

 E. Race Does Matter

  1. Racial classifications are based on racist generalizations.

  2. Students define race in terms of skin color, cultural, and ethnic backgrounds, while others express a more political perspective on the issue.

 F. It's a gender thang: Our sense of self develops based on our gender.

 G. We develop and modify our self-concept when we compare ourselves to others.

III. Self That We Communicate to Others

 A. Self disclosure is the process of providing others with information about the self.

 B. Self-disclosure concerns you—your thoughts, feelings and behaviors—or your intimates that have a significant bearing on who you are.

 C. Self-disclosure is most often used to refer to information that you normally keep hidden rather than simply to information that you have not previously revealed.

  1. Our attitudes, beliefs, and values make up a significant part of our self-concepts. When we disclose information about our values, beliefs and values, we are essentially revealing something about who we think we are.

  2. Self-disclosure reveals information about the self that others are unlikely to detect through other means.

  3. Self-disclosure is the process of intentionally and unintentionally providing others with information about the self (attitudes, beliefs, values, etc.) that is unlikely to be discovered through other means.

 D. We self-disclose in order to develop relationships.

 E. Our self-disclosure invites others to self-disclose to us.

 F. Self-disclosure should be monitored for appropriateness.

  1. Some people are extremely turned off by hearing too much too soon.

  2. It is not always safe to self-disclose to individuals with whom you are not well acquainted.

  3. Self-disclosure is fundamental to interpersonal closeness.

IV. Self That We Communicate to Self

 A. Self-talk, the inner conversations we have with ourselves, greatly influences our emotional well-being.

 B. We are always engaged in intrapersonal communication or self-talk.

 C. Intrapersonal communication influences our self-concept, self-esteem, and emotional state.

 D. Self-talk shapes how we see the world, how we see ourselves in relation to the world and how we see ourselves in relation to others in the world.

V. Evolving Self

 A. Change can be a wonderful thing.

 B. Change can be a necessary thing.

  1. Change has as its very nature transforming power.

  2. When things are not going right, they need to, ultimately, change.

 C. There are times in our lives where we have to change course.

Name: _____ *Section:* _____ *Date:* _____

4.5 Positives and Negatives

What is the difference between self-fulfilling prophecy and self-sabotage? When would each be used? Which do you utilize more often in your self-talk?

_____

_____

_____

_____

_____

_____

_____

_____

_____

_____

_____

_____

_____

_____

4.6 Race and Gender Matters

Films such as *White Man's Burden* portray a culture where African Americans have higher social status than Caucasians. Imagine that you live in such a society. What would be different? What would be the same?

_____

_____

_____

_____

_____

_____

Now imagine that you live in a culture that values female over male. What would be different? What would be the same?

_____

_____

_____

_____

_____

_____

_____

_____

_____

Name: _____ Section: _____ Date: _____

4.7 Heterosexism

After reading Dr. Gunn's essay on heterosexism, list and discuss other examples of heterosexism that are prevalent in modern society. In what ways can society work to improve the examples you listed?

_____

_____

_____

_____

_____

_____

_____

_____

_____

_____

_____

_____

_____

_____

_____

_____

_____

_____

Name: _____   Section: _____ Date: _____

Test Yourself

Match these vocabulary terms with the descriptions that best define them.

1. _____ Self

2. _____ Self-Fulfilling Prophecy

3. _____ Direct Definitions

4. _____ Self-Sabotage

5. _____ Particular Others

6. _____ Generalized Others

7. _____ Heterosexism

a. Arises out of negative self-talk

b. Intrapersonal communication

c. Communicate who are parents/society see us as

d. Assumption that everyone is heterosexual

e. Multidimensional product comprised of many internal and external factors

f. People most important to us as infants

g. Faceless group of rules and roles

chapter Five

Nonverbal Communication: Saying It Without Words

Chapter Outline

I. What is nonverbal communication?
  A. Nonverbal communication is the process of transporting messages through behaviors, physical characteristics and objects.
  B. Nonverbal communication is also about how we say things.
  C. Research shows that verbal symbols (words) are not as important to the meaning of a message as nonverbal cues or nonverbal behaviors.
    1. Thirty to 35 percent of meaning is carried by the words.
    2. 65 to 70 percent of meaning is carried by nonverbal cues.
II. Nonverbal communication has several specific characteristics.
  A. Nonverbal communication is culturally defined.
    1. Nonverbal are ambiguous.
    2. We get our meaning for nonverbal symbols from our culture.
  B. Nonverbal differences exist between women and men.
    1. Although men and women may share a common culture, their nonverbal behaviors tend to differ.
    2. The nonverbal behaviors of females usually differ from the nonverbal behaviors of males.
  C. Nonverbal communication often unconsciously shows feelings and attitudes.
    1. Our feelings and attitudes are often unconsciously transmitted through our nonverbal messages.
  D. Nonverbal communication may conflict with verbal communication.
    1. When our nonverbal messages are inconsistent with our verbal messages, we are sending mixed messages.
    2. Nonverbal and verbal communication are not at odds in all aspects.
    3. Nonverbal communication functions to reinforce, substitute for, and regulate verbal communication.
      a. There are instances where nonverbal communication functions to reinforce verbal messages.
      b. Nonverbal messages often substitute for spoken words.
      c. Nonverbal communication can manage our verbal interactions with others. Nonverbal behaviors can regulate the flow of conversation.

III. Nonverbal communication can be broken down into many different categories.
  A. Aesthetics refer to environmental factors and how they are manipulated to influence our feelings and emotions.
    1. Environmental factors include colors, lighting, spatial arrangement, and sounds.
    2. Olfactics relates to the perception of scents and smells.
    3. We attempt to control or influence the mood by controlling the setting.
  B. Artifacts are objects that we use to express our identities.
    1. These objects announce who we are or at least who we think we are.
    2. Our personal appearance does make a nonverbal statement.
    3. Artifacts help us to perform gender.
  C. Chronemics is how we use and handle time to communicate messages.
    1. As with other nonverbal behaviors, time and its significance are culturally defined.
      a. Most Western Europeans, Japanese and North Americans would probably consider punctuality as a sign of good manners.
      b. Native American Navajo believe that the time to start a ceremony or function is when the preparations for the ceremony are complete—whenever that might be (Hall, 1976).
    2. Power is communicated through the usage of time. The person in power tends to make you wait.
  D. Haptics is nonverbal communication that involves physical touch.
    1. Research on touch reiterates the importance of touch in our everyday lives.
    2. The use of touch is greatly influenced by our culture and gender.
  E. Kinesics refers to how we use body movements to communicate.
    1. We convey the majority of our nonverbal messages through facial expressions.
    2. Hand gestures are associated with power.
  F. Oculesics refers to eye behavior.
  G. Physical appearance refers to an individual's physical qualities.
    1. The American culture strongly emphasizes physical appearance.
    2. Skin color, hairstyle, sex, and size, are characteristics that we generally notice as soon as we look at a person.
  H. Paralanguage, sometimes referred to as vocalics, is how we say what we say.
    1. Paralanguage includes sounds such as grunts, groans, moans, and sighs, as well as vocal codes such as volume (loudness), rate (the speed at which you speak), pitch (the highness or lowness of your voice), and inflection (the change in pitch and volume of your voice).
    2. Vocal codes tell people how to perceive us.
  I. Proxemics is the study of how we use space to communicate.
    1. From your skin to 18 inches outward is your intimate space. This is space is usually reserved for those with whom we are intimate.
    2. Personal space extends from 18 inches to 4 feet.
    3. We conduct formal interactions within our social space, which extends from 4 feet to about 12 feet.
    4. Public space extends from 12 feet and beyond.

Name: _____ Section: _____ Date: _____

5.1 Grooming Habits

Make a list of the grooming procedures you go through in the mornings (makeup, hair, cologne, etc). Next, make list of your grooming habits before a first date. Compare and contrast your habits for both instances.

Morning Grooming Habits	Before Date Grooming Habits

Questions

1. How does context affect the amount of grooming?

2. Why might there be a difference in time spent grooming between men and women?

3. What might the gender differences be regarding body modification? Who exercises more? Who gets more plastic surgery? Why?

Name: _____ *Section:* _____ *Date:* _____

5.2 Poise

Have you ever wondered how much a person's body language affects you? Take a few minutes and write the different impressions you might form about someone who is slouching? Standing up straight? What leads you to these conclusions? Use specific examples.

_____

_____

_____

_____

_____

_____

_____

_____

_____

_____

_____

_____

_____

_____

_____

_____

_____

5.3 Conformity

Watch your favorite television program or movie and study the artifacts worn by the actors, and then answer the following questions.

1. Was there a common theme running through the show/movie in regards to artifacts?

2. Look in the mirror and through your closet. Do your artifactual choices resemble those in the show/movie? Do the similarities have any effect on your enjoyment of the show?

3. Do your friends dress similar to you? Did you dress similar when you met or acquire each other's tastes in artifacts? Do you feel more comfortable with people that look or dress like you? Have you ever been made fun of for a fashion faux pas? Did you ever wear that outfit/jewelry/hairstyle again?

4. Sit in a public place and watch groups and dyads. Do groups of friends dress similarly? What about couples? Why might this be? Did you notice any groups or couples that dressed differently? Did you find it odd?

Name: _____ *Section:* _____*Date:* _____

5.4 Permanent Structures and Space

In the space provided below answer the following questions. Compare your answers to your classmates. What does your apartment or house say about you? The location, size, etc? What would a new friend discover about you if they were to enter your home?

_____

_____

_____

_____

_____

_____

_____

_____

_____

_____

_____

_____

_____

_____

_____

_____

_____

_____

5.5 Nonverbal Communication and Chat Rooms

Go online to a generic chat room (such as current events, health and wellness, or music). Watch the conversation for several minutes.

When watching the conversation, what did you notice about the way language was structured? What nonverbal behaviors are lacking (body communication, artifacts, etc.)? Did the online participants attempt to make up for the lack of nonverbal cues? How?

Observe an online romantic chat room (love, flirting, etc.). Watch the conversation. How do these participants make up for the lack of nonverbals? Does anyone take it too far? Is there a possibility of deceit?

How do the participants make up for the lack of paralanguage? Do they use emoticons, special language/internet "lingo," or abbreviations? Would a newcomer to the forum have an immediate understanding of the language being used, or is there an easy reference section to help them acclimate to the discussion board.

Name: _____ *Section:* _____ *Date:* _____

5.6 Categories of Nonverbal Communication

For each category of nonverbal communication, give an example of how the communication process could be helped or hindered.

Aesthetics: _____

_____

Artifacts: _____

_____

Chronemics: _____

_____

Haptics: _____

_____

Kinesics: _____

_____

Paralanguage: _____

_____

Physical Appearance: _____

_____

Proxemics: _____

_____

Oculesics: _____

_____

5.7 Communication through Artifacts

After reading the section on artifacts in the textbook, think about what the artifacts you wear communicate about you. Make a list of artifacts and what you think they say about you. After you have completed your list, ask a friend what they think each of your artifacts mean. Compare and contrast differences and similarities.

Artifact	Your Opinion	Friend's Opinion

Name: _____ *Section:* _____ *Date:* _____

5.8 Mixed Messages

Analyze a conversation where you either gave or received mixed messages (nonverbal and verbal messages contradicting one another). Did the verbal or nonverbal message have more weight in the conversation? How did you (or other participants) resolve the mixed messages? What will you do differently next time?

_____

_____

_____

_____

_____

_____

_____

_____

_____

_____

_____

_____

_____

_____

_____

_____

_____

Name: _____ *Section:* _____ *Date:* _____

Test Yourself

Match these vocabulary terms with the descriptions that best define them.

1. _____ Mixed Messages   a. Eye behavior

2. _____ Aesthetics   b. Environmental factors

3. _____ Artifacts   c. Vocal variations

4. _____ Chronemics   d. Physical touch

5. _____ Haptics   e. Inconsistent verbal and nonverbal messages

6. _____ Kinesics   f. Personal presentation

7. _____ Paralanguage   g. Time

8. _____ Physical Appearance   h. Physical space

9. _____ Proxemics   i. Personal objects

10. _____ Oculesics   j. Body movements

chapter six

Interpersonal Communication: Moving Beyond Self to Connect with Another

Chapter Outline

I. Definition of Interpersonal Communication

    A. Interpersonal communication is the interaction between at least two individuals within a sociohistorical context, which is affected by each person's environment, experiences, self-concept, general worldview, and previous interactions with each other.

    B. Interpersonal communication is simply moving beyond yourself to consider another person's needs, perspectives, and interpretations of your words and actions in the context of your relationship over time.

II. Perspective

    A. The great thing about perspective is it will be there whether you verbalize or acknowledge it or not.

    B. There is power in getting to know who you are, what your perspective is, when it came to be what it is, where your perspective comes from, how it came to be, and why it is what it is.

    C. We often think that we are the world and everything centers on us, our desires, our needs, our feelings, our concerns, our fears, etc.

        1. Ethnocentrism, the belief that everything centers around our culture's way of doing and being.

        2. Egocentrism, the belief that everything centers around "me" and my way of doing and being.

III. Worldview

    A. Worldview is basically how you see the world, your vantage point.

    B. Individualistic worldview is one in which the focus is on the individual advancing regardless of the cost to the collective.

    C. Collectivistic worldview is one in which the focus is on the good of the collective regardless of the expense to the individual.

IV. Individuals within a Collective

    A. Each of us is a part of multiple groups, all of which are a part of the larger world system in which we exist.

B. In our society we are taught that certain characteristics or group affiliations should be focused on more than others. We have to decide the level of importance we will place on our group memberships and the role they will play in shaping our identities.

C. Generalizations don't work when we are dealing with specific individuals within a collective or collectives. Many factors will influence those individual choices, including acceptance of the responsibilities that come along with freedom and rights.

V. Interpersonal Communication across Relationship Types

A. Family Communication

   1. Family means different things to different people.

   2. Family is complex because of the complexity of our society.

   3. In our families, we have rules of some sort.

B. Peer Communication and Friendship

   1. Interactions with our peers and developing friendships are an important part of interpersonal communication.

   2. It is in our relationships with our peers that we really begin to explore our use of communication strategies.

   3. In friendships, there are slightly different rules than the ones used with someone "off the street" or someone to whom you aren't connected.

   4. Friends serve several functions in our lives.

      a. Identity Needs

      b. Support and Encouragement

      c. Companionship

      d. Honest Feedback or Constructive Criticism

C. Romantic Communication

   1. Trends suggest that race and gender have a greater impact on some aspects of communication than others, but the assumption that there is no impact and no difference should not be made automatically.

   2. There are many factors that can influence whether or not we disclose information to others, allow ourselves to become intimate, and the role our communication competence plays in it all.

   3. Romantic communication, like all of the other types of communication, requires that we work on being effective.

D. Interpersonal Communication Climate

   1. Interpersonal communication climate is the way people feel when they interact with each other.

   2. Defensive behavior is defined as that behavior that occurs when an individual perceives threat or anticipates threat in the group.[1]

   3. The defensive mode prevents a listener from concentrating on the message.

---

[1](Gibb, 1988).

4. Gibb analyzed numerous taped discussions and identified six pairs of supportive and defensive categories.
   a. Evaluation/Description
      i. Evaluative language usually illustrates us as good or bad, right or wrong.
      ii. Descriptive communication describes behaviors without evaluating whether they are good or bad, right or wrong.
   b. Control/Problem Orientation
      i. Control language attempts to manipulate the listener into accepting the speaker's point of view.
      ii. Problem oriented language solicits collaborative decision making.
   c. Strategy/Spontaneity
      i. Strategy communication plan to dupe or manipulate their listeners by keeping their motives hidden.
      ii. Spontaneous speech is not contrived.
   d. Neutrality/Empathy
      i. Neutral speech communicates a lack of concern about the listener.
      ii. Empathetic speech communicates to me that I am worthwhile.
   e. Superiority/Equality
      i. Equality language communicates congruency.
   f. Certainty Provisionalism
      i. Certainty/superiority language is absolute and does not allow for further discussion.
      ii. A speaker using provisional language communicates a willingness to listen, a willingness to hear other perspectives and criticisms.

Name: _____ *Section:* _____ *Date:* _____

6.1 Standpoint and Perceptions

Revisit the activities in Chapter 1 with regard to Standpoint Theory (1.1 and 1.8). How does your standpoint effect your perceptions of others in interpersonal communication? If your standpoint changes, will your perceptions change? In what way?

_____

_____

_____

_____

_____

_____

_____

_____

_____

_____

_____

_____

_____

_____

_____

_____

_____

_____

6.2 How do I be "ME" if I am also "THEM"?

After reading the section in Chapter 6 about "Individuals within a Collective", think about what collective groups you are involved in. What are the collective values of that group? Are they similar or different to your own personal values? What challenges do different individual and collective values present?

My Values:

Group Values:

Challenges Present:

Name: _____ *Section:* _____ *Date:* _____

6.3 Ya Gotta Have Friends

Review the functions of friendship in Chapter 6. Reflect on your relationship with your closest friend. Examine and explain the ways that your friend meets each function.

Identity Needs:

Support and Encouragement:

Companionship:

Honest Feedback or Constructive Criticism:

6.4 Cross-Culture Friendships

Read the essay titled "Communicating Friendship across Cultural Lines: From Stereotype to Sacrifice" in Chapter 6. Reflect on a friendship you have had with a person of a different race or culture. Did you have a similar experience, or one opposite that of the author? How did you and your friend work through any cultural differences that arose throughout your friendship?

_____

_____

_____

_____

_____

_____

_____

_____

_____

_____

_____

_____

_____

_____

_____

_____

Name: _____ *Section:* _____ *Date:* _____

6.5 Family Rules!

What are the rules (both spoken and unspoken) in your family with regard to communication? Do the rules change depending on the participants (sibling to sibling, parent to child, parent to parent, etc.)? Are the rules the same for all situations, or do they change as the interaction type changes (arguments, joking, everyday conversation, etc.)?

_____

_____

_____

_____

_____

_____

_____

_____

_____

_____

_____

_____

_____

_____

_____

_____

_____

6.6 Romance and Culture

Read the dialogue in the romantic communication section of Chapter 6. Thinking critically, rewrite the conversation from the perspective of a person involved in a same-sex romantic relationship. How is the conversation different? Does this break gender molds and stereotypes, or contribute to them?

_____

_____

_____

_____

_____

_____

_____

_____

_____

_____

_____

_____

_____

_____

Name: _____ *Section:* _____ *Date:* _____

Test Yourself

Match these vocabulary terms with the descriptions that best define them.

1. _____ Individualistic Worldview
2. _____ Collectivistic Worldview
3. _____ Perspective
4. _____ Individual within a Collective
5. _____ Ethnocentrism
6. _____ Egocentrism
7. _____ Defensive Behavior
8. _____ Evaluative Language
9. _____ Descriptive Language
10. _____ Interpersonal Communication

a. Communication between people

b. Occurs when threat is perceived

c. Focus on individual differences within a group

d. Focus on the individual

e. Description without judgement

f. Belief in your own superiority

g. Your personal outlook on situations

h. Focus on the group

i. Description with judgement

j. Belief in one culture's superiority

chapter Seven

In Black and White: Race and Communication

Chapter Outline

I. Introduction
   A. There are numerous factors that influence the development of communication patterns: including the family of origin, life experiences, level of education, socioeconomic level, and the communication norms of the communities they belong to.
   B. Communication patterns also differ by cultural affiliation and race.
   C. Cultural groups share speech codes: distinct systems of communication rules, norms, and patterns that guide their communication behaviors with others.
   D. A speech code is a system of communication rules, norms, and patterns that guide communication behaviors with others.
      1. Research shows that speech codes differ by race, and that this is the cause of many interracial tensions.
      2. The differences between black people and white people are based on two distinct speech codes: two different sets of communication rules for what is acceptable and normal.
II. Definitions: What Is Race?
   A. The concept of "race" is defined by people, not by biology.
      1. Different cultures define race differently, based on history and tradition.
      2. There is no genetic difference among humans that could explain all the attributes we associate with race.
   B. Race is a collection of beliefs, values, experiences, history, practices, and social, political, and economic positionality.
   C. Communication patterns adopted by groups of people both reflect and create the collective experiences of each cultural group, and provide for shared identity.
   D. Within all races, there are many different ethnicities and cultural groups.
III. Guiding Principles
   A. Different does not equal wrong.
      1. Each culture has its own, unique communication system and patterns, and each is valid.
      2. There is significant difference within groups, as well as among groups.

B. Cultures are dynamic.

   1. Racial identities are not static.

   2. Definitions of race change.

C. Cultural competence is a process.

   1. Cultural competence is the ability to communicate effectively with people from a cultural background that is different from your own.

   2. Learning to be culturally competent takes some effort, self-discovery, and often a little discomfort, but the rewards go beyond just the personal benefit of becoming a more effective communicator.

D. Learning about others helps self-understanding.

E. Apprehension about racial differences is normal.

   1. Much of our self identity is based on race and culture.

   2. Our race does not define who we are, but the attitudes, values, and beliefs of our racial culture do influence our communication patterns.

F. Overcoming ethnocentrism is central.

   1. Ethnocentrism is the use of your own culture as the standard to measure others. It assumes that one culture is superior to another.

   2. Resisting ethnocentrism means that you are able to stop and consider another person's point of view, based on their cultural or racial norms.

G. Understanding does not mean you agree.

IV. Communication Patterns by Race

A. Language Use

   1. Black people tend to be creative with language, and use words and sayings that have specific meanings to members of the group: a shared code that reinforces shared identity.

   2. White people tend to use language literally, which is the use of words that have a specific, dictionary definition.

   3. Possible interpretations:

      a. Black people may think that white people are stiff and formal, and white people may think black people are not using correct English.

      b. We all recognize that language usage is cultural and that people use and interpret language in different ways.

      c. We realize that shared code is a way to create and reinforce a shared identity, and many groups, both black and white, use this as a tool to maintain close ties.

B. Sequencing

   1. Many black people organize and present their ideas in a weblike or circular fashion, and rely on examples to communicate an idea. This style of thinking and communicating has been identified in a number of cultures, not just in black culture.

   2. Many white people organize their thoughts in a linear fashion, usually in time sequence. An idea is communicated by presenting it from beginning to end, and staying directly on the topic.

3. Possible interpretations:
   a. Black people may think that white people are boring and dry, or too narrow-minded to see how examples are inter-connected, and white people may think that black people are disorganized.
   b. We all recognize that people may organize and communicate their thoughts in different, and valid, ways.

C. Eye Contact
   1. Eye contact is an important part of face-to-face communication, and so is the absence of eye contact.
   2. Many black people and white people share some cultural beliefs about the interpretation of eye contact: mainly that direct eye contact indicates honesty and respect, and the lack of it may mean someone is lying or hiding something.
   3. There are some differences in the way eye contact is used in conversations.
      a. Some black people maintain direct eye contact while they are speaking, and look away while listening.
      b. Some white people are the opposite: they maintain direct eye contact while they are listening, and avert their eyes when speaking.
   4. Possible interpretations:
      a. Black people may think they are being stared down by white people when they are talking, or looked down on, and white people may think black people are showing disrespect or aren't paying attention when they are talking.
      b. We all recognize that people learn eye contact behaviors from their families and communities, and have different ideas about when eye contact is appropriate.

D. Emotional Expressiveness
   1. Emotional expressiveness is the use of inflection, vocal range, rhythm, emphasis, and tone when speaking.
      a. Blacks tend to be emotionally expressive in their speech, and value authentic displays of emotion in public.
      b. Whites tend to be more reserved in their speech, and value self-control when displaying emotions in public.
   2. Possible interpretations:.
      a. Black people could think white people are cold-hearted or not authentic, and white people could think that black people are dramatic.
      b. We could all recognize that our rules for what is and is not acceptable in public communication are cultural, and that we should not use our own cultural communication practices to evaluate others.
      c. We should be aware that emotional expressiveness can be influenced by many factors in addition to race.

E. Taking Turns
   1. Turn-taking refers to who speaks (and when) and who listens (and when) in a one-on-one or group conversation.

    2. Possible interpretations:

        a. Blacks may perceive whites as passive or not interested, and whites may perceive blacks as rude or aggressive.

        b. We all recognize that turn-taking is a practice that results from cultural communication patterns.

  F. Assertive Language

    1. Some black people tend to use assertive, powerful language when they speak.

    2. Some white people tend to use language that is less assertive, by either softening word choice or tone.

    3. Possible interpretations:

        a. White people may think black people are aggressive or threatening, and black people may think white people are weak or fearful.

        b. We all recognize that black people and white people follow the communications rules of their cultural group, and we should consider speech codes when we interpret others' communication.

        c. Assertive communication is not necessarily an act of aggression and less assertive communication is not necessarily a sign of weakness.

  G. Topics of Conversation

    1. Many white people believe that asking another person about jobs, family, or other personal topics is a way to make a friendly introduction, even when they meet someone for the first time.

    2. Many black people regard personal topics inappropriate in initial conversations with people they do not know.

    3. Possible interpretations:

        a. Black people may think that white people are asking something that is too personal, and whites may think that blacks are unfriendly.

        b. We all recognize that different cultural groups have different ideas about what topics are acceptable and which are intrusive.

V. Similarities

  A. Cultural understanding broadens our cultural competence, and we become more effective communicators.

  B. Many factors influence communication styles, including how someone was raised, in what community, socioeconomic level, gender, and age among others. Race does not tell the whole story.

  C. Race is learned, and racial communication systems are also learned.

Name: _____ *Section:* _____*Date:* _____

7.1 Your Own Definition of Race

In the space provided, write your definition of race.

_____

_____

_____

_____

_____

_____

_____

Now, in small groups, discuss your definition of race. How does your definition differ from that of your classmates? Does your group believe race is important? Why are we so quick to judge others based on their race?

_____

_____

_____

_____

_____

_____

_____

_____

7.2 Communication by Race and the Movies

Watch the film "Love and Basketball" and write your observations about how the different races use communication. Next, watch the film "Remember the Titans" and write your observations about how the different races use communication. Compare your observations with that of your classmates.

"Love and Basketball"	"Remember the Titans"

Similarities from classmates _____

_____

_____

_____

_____

_____

_____

Name: _____ Section: _____ Date: _____

7.3 How Do You Communicate?

For three days, observe how you use communication. Pay attention to how you communicate when you interact with others. After three days, reflect on what you noticed about your nonverbal and verbal behaviors when communicating with individuals of your same ethnicity and individuals from different ethnicities. Was you behavior the same or did it differ? If you wanted to improve your communication, what steps would you take?

_____

_____

_____

_____

_____

_____

_____

_____

_____

_____

_____

_____

_____

_____

_____

7.4 Connotation and Denotation

Many words have more than one definition. This is especially true when dealing with slang words, and politically correct terminology. Think of some words that are in common usage when referring to race categories. Make a list of their denotative (dictionary) meanings, and their connotative (emotionally charged) meanings. Then explain why it is important to "mind what you say."

Terms in Use	Denotative Meaning	Connotative Meaning

It is important to understand the meaning behind what you say because

_____

_____

Name: _____   Section: _____ Date: _____

7.5 Acceptable and Normal

Think about differences between your race/culture and that of others. Make a list of what is considered "acceptable" and "normal" in your race/culture that might seem unusual or atypical in another race/culture. Then make a list of things that seem "acceptable" and "normal" in a race/culture different from your own, but seem out of place in your race/culture.

My Race/Culture	Other Races/Cultures

7.6 Tribal Differences

Chapter 7 discusses the fact that there are different "tribes" within the black and white communities (e.g.-there are different groups of white people, and different groups of black people). List some of these "tribes" for each race, and discuss what you think makes them different from another "tribe" of the same race.

Tribe or Group	Difference from Other Groups within That Race

Test Yourself

Match these vocabulary terms with the descriptions that best define them.

1. _____ Blacks

2. _____ Whites

3. _____ Latinos

4. _____ Race

5. _____ Dynamism

6. _____ Cultural Competence

7. _____ Ethnocentrism

8. _____ Literal Language

9. _____ Sequencing

a. Ability to communicate effectively with people of cultural backgrounds not your own

b. Words that have a specific, dictionary definition

c. European-Americans

d. Organization of speech patterns

e. Using your own culture to measure others

f. Inflection, vocal range, rhythm, emphasis, and tone when speaking

g. African Americans

h. Racial identities are not static

i. Hispanic Americans

chapter Eight

Small Group Communication as a Social Concern

Chapter Outline

I. What Is Small Group?
   A. Small groups consist of three to five interdependent individuals who communicate with one another to accomplish a common goal.
   B. In the small group context, members must be committed to accomplishing a shared goal.
      * When there is no desire or attempt to work together, the gathering of individuals is considered a collection.[1]
   C. Small groups whose members have little or no demographic commonalties are heterogeneous groups.
   D. On the other hand, groups whose members share common interests, attitudes, levels of knowledge, and other demographics are homogeneous groups.
   E. Groups have norms that regulate how members are expected to communicate and behave within the group context.
      1. Some norms are implied and some are explicitly stated.
      2. Explicit norms are rules of behavior that are expressed verbally or that may be put in writing.
      3. Implicit norms are the understood and expected behaviors of the group.
II. Multiple Kinds of Groups
   A. Groups vary in characteristics and concerns.
   B. Social groups seek to accomplish a recreational or social end.
      1. The common interest can be any number of things, including a hobby, a sport, scholastic aptitude, or a profession.
      2. Social groups include fraternities, sororities, athletic teams, car clubs, motorcycle clubs, chess clubs, honors clubs, singing groups, and the list goes on.

---

[1] (Wilson, 1999).

C. Self-help groups provide support to individuals who need help dealing with some aspect of their personal lives.

　1. Also readily known as support groups, therapy groups, or encounter groups, self-help groups provide their members with the opportunity to congregate and discuss their common problem, issue, or life circumstance.

　2. Self-help groups include Alcoholics Anonymous, Weight Watchers, Overeaters Anonymous, etc.

D. Learning groups enable individuals to enhance their knowledge and skills in a particular area.

　1. Members seek or share information.

　2. A college study group is a prime example of a group organized to provide members the opportunity to advance their knowledge.

　3. Learning groups can exist as faith-based study groups, groups of new employees in an orientation session, or seasoned employees in a training seminar.

E. Service groups provide their members with the opportunity to show goodwill.

　1. Members find satisfaction in helping each other as well as nonmembers.

　2. Service groups may focus on one particular type of issue or problem.

　3. Service organizations such as the Lions Club often provide needy individuals with eyeglasses, hearing aids, and other supplies that will increase their quality of life.

F. Work groups focus on accomplishing specific goals or tasks for associations, companies, organizations, faith groups, and institutions.

　1. These groups may be established to perform their tasks routinely, or they may be established to perform on an as needed basis.

　2. Committees are work groups that form as a result of the needs of a larger group or the needs of an individual in power.

　　a. Committees that form and carry out a specific task within a given time are ad hoc committees.

　　b. Standing committees form so that they can routinely carry out a specific function. These committees can exist as long as the institution exists.

　3. Teams are also considered work groups.

III. Fallen Star—A Problem with Cohesion

A. Cohesion is a commitment and attraction to the collective identity of the group.

B. When groups lack cohesion, something has interrupted the group's closeness.

C. Cohesive groups are much more productive.

D. Irving Janis (1977) developed the theory of groupthink, which essentially says that some groups are unable to rationally make decisions because individual group members are too close to each other.

　1. There are several factors that may lead to groupthink.

　2. Groups suffer from groupthink when they are *cut off from the larger society.*

　3. Groups may suffer from groupthink when the group *lacks ethical leadership.*

IV. Can't We All Just Get Along?

A. Conflict arises when the needs, ideas, and/or opinions of one or more group members are incongruent.

B. Some type of conflict is bound to arise in the group context.

C. It is important to realize that not all conflict is disruptive.

    1. Conflict can fuel some very energetic debates, yielding constructive results.

    2. When group members understand that conflict is natural, discussions are much more open.

    3. When group members view conflict as competition, discussions become battlegrounds.

D. In order to minimize conflict within a group, members should keep the discussions focused on the issues and not the individuals.

E. There is a basic problem-solving model that will streamline the time and effort used in group problem-solving.

    1. Define the problem.

        a. Questions of fact deal with whether something is true, or to what degree something is factual.

        b. Questions of value assess the worth of an idea, object, or individual.

        c. Questions of policy deal with how things "ought" to be.

    2. Research and analyze the problem.

    3. Establish guidelines or rules that the group must follow in order to reach a decision.

        a. Make checklist so that each group member is fully aware of the standards that they must follow. If a proposed solution does not meet the standards, it cannot be the accepted solution.

        b. Rank the standards so group members have a sense which standard is most important to follow.

    4. List and evaluate possible alternatives.

        a. Brainstorming is a way to solicit alternatives.

        b. These members would prefer the Nominal Group Technique (NGT) as a means of generating alternatives. The NGT allows members to generate ideas silently and then have their ideas recorded on the board, the overhead, or a flipchart.

    5. Select the best alternative and implement it.

V. Group Membership and Role Emergence

A. Group members are motivated to join based on a variety of individual reasons.

    1. Attraction to others in the group–Individuals may join groups solely because of physical attraction to other group members.

    2. Attraction to the group's activities–People who are attracted to a group's activities may enjoy aspects of the tasks involved, but they may not truly value the group's primary goal.

    3. Attraction to the group's goals–Members who are attracted to a group's goals are often more highly committed to achievement and to getting along with other group members. One of the most important predictors of a group's success is whether or not its members are attracted to the primary goals of the group.

    4. Attraction to being affiliated with the group–Some individuals join groups solely because they want to be associated with that group. They do not really care about the tasks or goals of the group, and they do not really want to get

involved with the issues or other group members. They may occasionally attend group meetings. Members who join groups solely for reasons of affiliation will often present problems for the group.

  5. Attraction to needs outside of the group–Some members are attracted to groups for reasons not at all associated with the goals and tasks of the group. They may have no particular interest in the other group members but may join only to bolster their resumes or because it is a socially accepted thing to do. These members are often poor group members. They are often unreliable, may rarely attend meetings and/or may be disruptive if they do attend.

B. During this process, individuals will gravitate toward various roles.

  1. In the study of group process, the concept of role refers to the part that an individual plays within a group.

  2. Some roles are said to be formal.

   a. These formal roles are specifically assigned by the group and often carry a title like president, secretary or chairperson.

   b. When a formal role is assigned and accepted by an individual, there is said to be role stability.

  3. Other roles are said to be informal.

   a. Informal roles are more naturally occurring and are based more on function (accomplishing a specific task) than position (overall governing of the group).

   b. For example, a person may attempt to provide leadership around working on a certain project without holding a formal position within the organization. Informal roles are not always leadership positions, however.

   c. For example, if a group becomes engaged in a heated discussion, the function required may be that of a tension reliever.   Someone may need to tell a joke or otherwise step in to lighten the mood if needed.

   d. Another function might be that a group member volunteers to serve as a recorder on occasion, in order to document important ideas that are being discussed.

   e. A final example might be when a group member who knows of information that would be of particular interest to the group serves as an information provider.

  4. Roles emerge over time in what has been characterized as a trial and error process.

  5. Members will provide feedback on whether an individual's behaviors are acceptable.

Name: _____ Section: _____ Date: _____

8.1 Setting Rules for Working in Groups

Researchers have found that nearly sixty percent of individuals who work in groups disdain group work. You are asked to participate in a group whose task is to organize and run homecoming. In the space provided, brainstorm rules for your group, a group goal, and a timeline that you and your group members should follow.

_____

_____

_____

_____

_____

_____

_____

_____

_____

_____

_____

_____

_____

_____

_____

_____

8.2 You and Your Groups

Review the different types of groups discussed in the chapter. Categorize the various clubs, activities, organizations that you participate in, according to the definition of the group. Is there any one group that your activities don't fit under? Why did you join these groups?

_____

_____

_____

_____

_____

_____

_____

_____

_____

_____

_____

_____

_____

_____

Name: _____ *Section:* _____ *Date:* _____

8.3 College and Conflict

Many college students participate in groups in which conflict is inevitable.   Recall a time that you participated in a group with conflict. How do college students deal with conflict? Does your experience with group conflict differ from your experience with interpersonal conflict? What suggestions do you have in order for groups to effectively deal with conflict?

_____

_____

_____

_____

_____

_____

_____

_____

_____

_____

_____

_____

_____

_____

_____

_____

8.4 Group Appropriateness

List and discuss when it is appropriate for each type of group to form. What types of functions would these groups serve? Offer examples.

Social Groups: _____

_____

Self-help Groups: _____

_____

Learning Groups: _____

_____

Service Groups _____

_____

Work Groups: _____

_____

Committees: _____

_____

Standing Committees: _____

_____

Name: _____ *Section:* _____ *Date:* _____

8.5 Groupthink

Based on the definition of groupthink, is there a time when groupthink would be appropriate? If so, when? Why would groupthink be appropriate in certain situations, but not in others?

_____

_____

_____

_____

_____

_____

_____

_____

_____

_____

_____

_____

_____

_____

_____

_____

_____

_____

8.6 Who Decides What Is Normal?

Using the types of groups from Activity 7.4, make a list of implicit and explicit norms that you think each group would utilize.

Social Groups: _____

_____

Self-help Groups: _____

_____

Learning Groups: _____

_____

Service Groups: _____

_____

Work Groups: _____

_____

Committees: _____

_____

Standing Committees: _____

_____

Name: _____ *Section:* _____ *Date:* _____

8.7 Rules of Attraction

Discuss reasons why people would be attracted to groups. Cite examples for each rule of attraction.

Attraction to Others in the Group: _____

_____

Attraction to the Group's Activities: _____

_____

Attraction to the Group's Goals: _____

_____

Attraction to Being Affiliated with the Group: _____

_____

Attraction to Needs Outside of the Group: _____

_____

Name: _____ Section: _____ Date: _____

Test Yourself

Match these vocabulary terms with the descriptions that best define them.

1. _____ Social Groups
2. _____ Self-help Groups
3. _____ Learning Groups
4. _____ Service Groups
5. _____ Work Groups
6. _____ Committees
7. _____ Teams
8. _____ Groupthink
9. _____ Implicit Norms
10. _____ Explicit Norms

a. Focus on task accomplishments

b. Specialized work groups

c. Rules of behavior that are discussed

d. Focus on knowledge enhancement

e. Focus on recreational goals

f. Occurs with too much cohesion

g. Provide support

h. Rules of behavior that are implied

i. Sub-work groups

j. Focus on displays of goodwill

chapter Nine

Leadership Styles:
Gender and Cultural Differences

Chapter Outline

I. Gender and Leadership Styles

    A. Research shows that women and men differ in the type of leadership roles they undertake within work groups.

        1. Men exhibit more overall leadership and task leadership characteristics.

        2. Women exhibit more social leadership characteristics.

        3. Men and women have various leadership styles.

    B. Terminology Associated with Leadership

        1. A *leader* as defined by Bennis (1989) is a person(s) who shares some, if not all, of the following ingredients: (1) Guiding vision of what they want to accomplish, (2) Passion for promises of life, combined with a very particular passion for a vocation, a profession, a course of action, and (3) Integrity which consists of self-knowledge, candor, and maturity.

        2. *Leadership styles* as defined by Hersey and Blanchard (1991) cited in Brookbank: Consistent behavior patterns perceived by others that leaders use when they are working with and through those people.

        3. *Gender traits* as defined by Brookbank (1991): Personal characteristics that have been historically, culturally, and socially analogous with a specific gender. Examples of masculine gender traits include assertiveness, self-confidence, personal courage, organizational loyalty, and discipline, just to name a few. Examples of feminine gender traits include compassion, nurturance, organizational skills, and attention to "housekeeping" details, just to name a few.

II. Leadership Characteristics

    A. Men and women exhibit different leadership characteristics.

        1. Most men are task-oriented. Men tend to focus on completion of the job without much consideration for the people involved.

        2. Most women are more concerned about how the people involved feel with the completion of the job.

    B. Coping with stress on the job provides an example of perhaps one of the biggest differences between men and women.

    1. Men become increasingly focused and withdrawn when confronted with a stressful situation.

    2. Women become increasingly overwhelmed and emotionally involved.

C. The differences in leadership styles between men and women show that males are self-interested and focused on status, while females are interested in others and focused on connection.

D. There are differences in how males and females are evaluated as leaders.

III. Gender differences in conflict management is an important issue to study because there will be times of conflict in organizations.

A. Conflict management between men and women is often dictated by what society has established as traditional male and female roles.

B. Each gender will handle conflict a certain way because they are expected to choose those behaviors just because of their gender.

C. Ethics plays a role in conflict management. One part of ethics is morality and fairness, and men and women handle this part differently.

D. Research shows five conflict-handling styles: competition, collaboration, avoidance, compromise, and accommodation.

    1. Competition means to win at the expense of others.

        a. This strategy is very uncooperative and very assertive, but it is not necessarily hostile or obviously aggressive.

        b. It is used to meet one's own goals.

    2. Collaboration means to meet both parties' needs.

        a. It is concerned with finding new options and joint problem-solving.

        b. This strategy is both very cooperative and very assertive.

    3. Avoidance means failing to take a position in a conflict.

        a. People who use this strategy refuse to discuss the issues, which might be illustrated by leaving the room or attempting to change the subject.

        b. It is very uncooperative and very unassertive.

    4. Compromise means only partially meeting both parties' needs.

        a. It is a give-and-take method, and it reaches the middle ground in finding solutions.

        b. Both parties get a portion of what they want, but they do not get exactly what they want.

        c. This strategy is cooperative and assertive.

    5. Accommodation means rejecting one's goals for those of the other party.

        a. It allows for the satisfaction of others, and it can be either total agreement, without any hostility toward the other party, or it can be surrender.

        b. This strategy is very cooperative and not assertive.

E. Differentiation is defined as: raising the conflict issue, spending time and energy clarifying the positions, pursuing reasons behind the positions, and acknowledging the severity of the differences.

   * Differentiation is the process done in substantive conflict.

IV. Leadership and Minorities

    A. Suggestions for incorporating both race and gender in policies and practices that can promote equity in a diverse society seemed to be the question of the day!

    B. Equity must become a proactive goal in the schools and in the workplace, rather than a reactive response to wrongs committed.

    C. Gender and racial biases are still prevalent in the workplace.

    D. Minority Women

        1. Black women especially have been virtually ignored as a topic of sociological inquiry.

        2. African-American women have traditionally been relegated to subordinate positions in society that have affected the manner in which their leadership has emerged (Collins, 1991).

        3. The remainder of this discussion focuses on some areas that pose a challenge for the African-American female simply because of her race and gender.

        4. These areas are: (1) lack of mentors; (2) perception of legislation designed to uplift the status of minorities in the United States; and (3) the lack of respect given to African American female leaders.

    E. Society has an investment in seeing that people conform to expected sex-role behavior.

Name: _____ *Section:* _____ *Date:* _____

9.1 Examining Your Leadership in Groups

Explain a situation where you had to have a certain leadership role in a group. Explain what you had to do in order to achieve your goal and what things were sacrificed to get the job done.

_____

_____

_____

_____

_____

_____

_____

_____

_____

_____

_____

_____

_____

_____

_____

_____

_____

_____

_____

9.2 Couples and Cultural Roles

Find at least two different couples of different cultures and find out what roles the men and women play as leaders; how their social lives are different from those of the modern American cultural; and how they handle conflict. Write a brief summary of what you learned.

_____

_____

_____

_____

_____

_____

_____

_____

_____

_____

_____

_____

_____

_____

_____

_____

_____

Name: _____ *Section:* _____ *Date:* _____

9.3 Emerging Roles and Leadership[1]

Identify a recently formed group of at least five members to which you belong where informal leaders have emerged. In the space provided, identify the roles that each member of the group seems to play. Then answer the following questions: Is there a formal leader? Who are the informal leaders? How did they emerge? What is it that each does that leads you to believe that person is fulfilling leadership functions? Why was each of the other members of the group eliminated from informal leadership? Suppose the goal of group was changed? In what way might this affect the leadership of the group?

Member	Roles

[1]Adapted from L.E. Assante, *Student workbook: Communication for Verderbers* (10th Edition), (Belmont, CA: Wadsworth Publishing, 2002), 94.

9.4 Role Play

Review the list of groups that you are a member in (Activity 7.2). For each group, list what role(s) you play. What role are you most comfortable with? What role is the least comfortable for you? Why?

_____

_____

_____

_____

_____

_____

_____

_____

_____

_____

_____

_____

_____

_____

_____

_____

Name: _____ *Section:* _____ *Date:* _____

9.5 He Said/She Said

Using the list of characteristics for female and male leaders in Chapter 9 of the text-book, reflect on what leadership traits you bring to a group. Do you fit the gender categories discussed in the chapter, or do you have characteristics from both genders? Why is it important to think critically about the gender assignation for each trait?

_____

_____

_____

_____

_____

_____

_____

_____

_____

_____

_____

_____

_____

_____

_____

_____

_____

_____

9.6 Healthy Conflict

List examples for each type of conflict discussed in Chapter 9. Which type of conflict management is most appropriate for each example you list?

Competition: _____

_____

Collaboration: _____

_____

Avoidance: _____

_____

Compromise: _____

_____

Accommodation: _____

_____

Differentiation: _____

_____

Name: _____ *Section:* _____ *Date:* _____

9.7 Mediated Images

View a minimum of ten commercials played on various stations (sports, music videos, local stations, all-news stations, etc.). What roles are assigned for each gender in the commercials? Is one gender consistently portrayed in one way or another? Who is the intended audience of the commercial or the television program? Does the commercial have negative, positive, or neutral influences on this audience?

_____

_____

_____

_____

_____

_____

_____

_____

_____

_____

_____

_____

_____

_____

_____

_____

_____

_____

_____

Name: _____ *Section:* _____ *Date:* _____

Test Yourself

Match these vocabulary terms with the descriptions that best define them.

1. _____ Leader
2. _____ Leadership Styles
3. _____ Gender Traits
4. _____ Competition
5. _____ Collaboration
6. _____ Avoidance
7. _____ Compromise
8. _____ Accommodation
9. _____ Differentiation

a. Allowing the other person to win at your expense

b. Winning at the expense of others

c. Behavior patterns consistent with leaders

d. Raising the conflict issue

e. Partially meeting both parties needs

f. Person possessing a guiding vision

g. Fully meeting both parties needs

h. Socially constructed characteristics

i. Failing to take a position

chapter Ten

Ethically Speaking

Chapter Outline

I. Defining Ethics

  A. Individual ethics-our set of values which guide us in our daily decision making.

  B. Ethics-morals, beliefs, norms, and values that societies use to determine right from wrong.

II. The Basics: Freedom of Speech–A Highly Valued American Right

  A. There are four conditions for assessing the degree of the freedom of speech we have (Fraleigh, 1997).

    1. Freedom to Communicate without Fear of Government Sanction

      a. The freedom to communicate without fear of government sanction suggests that the government will not censor information.

      b. The freedom from compulsory speech means that we should not be required to say certain things.

    2. Freedom from Compulsory Speech

      a. The freedom to communicate without fear of government sanction suggests that the government will not censor information.

      b. The freedom from compulsory speech means that we should not be required to say certain things.

    3. Freedom of Access to Effective Channels of Communication

    4. Freedom from Government Domination of the Free Speech Environment

  B. Why is freedom of speech so critical?

    1. We defend and substantiate our right to the freedom of speech because it is critical to our system of "self-government" and it promotes "the discovery of truth" (Fraleigh, 1997).

    2. It encourages free will, independence, and freedom while affirming the premise that one person does not necessarily possess the moral right to stifle or suppress the ideas of another person!

  C. When do the courts tend to control speech?

    1. Safety and welfare of our society often takes precedence in the courts when the freedom of speech is in question.

    2. There are many questions about the responsibility a speaker has when provoking or encouraging an audience to perform an illegal act.

D. Communication and Morality

1. The moral absolute determines right and wrong from their perceived absolute truths.

2. This "absolute" is considering only one standard, *yours,* and no one else's.

3. Moral relativism is the notion that we may consider that there are other ethical systems that others choose and their choices are equally respected.

   a. Moral relativism brings difficulty to an already complex study of ethics in communications.

   b. Ethical communication suggests we are simultaneously expected to be able to respect others, affect another's behavior, and maintain our own psychological health.

E. An ethical audit is simply an appraisal of a situation or a potential situation that may challenge the morality of actions.

III. Ethical Communication Theories

A. Virtue ethics emphasizes the unity of acts and reasons.

1. Virtue ethics advocates that speakers communicate in a way that is not manipulating another.

2. Aristotle was concerned with the advancement of societal virtues like freedom, justice, courage, temperance, fairness, gentleness, and wisdom.

3. Aristotle's view would strongly suggest the ethical goal in communication would be to choose to find mutuality, middle ground, and a central point.

B. Taoist Ethics

1. The premise in Taoist ethics focuses on a vigorous ecology of values promoting the concept of natural balance.

2. Everything should exist only in harmony with someone or something else, hence the "yin-yang" concept.

   a. Where yin and yang are comparative opposites, interdependent, are supportive of each other, and can transform into one another.

   b. The communicators are unique and will clearly define their views.

C. Dialogic ethics is an understanding of how important it is to not devalue others by avoiding rhetorical manipulation and objectification.

1. A speaker might begin to think of their audience as merely valuable objects.

2. There are six characteristics of dialogue developed by Richard Johannesen (1990) that fit in this dialogic ethical theory: authenticity, inclusion, confirmation, present-ness, spirit of mutual equality, and a supportive climate.

IV. The Base of Our Ethical Guidelines

A. Egalitarianism is primarily concerned with the goal of social equality, fairness, and justice.

1. In this philosophy, an ethical speaker will be more concerned with fairness and equality than any other goal in their communication efforts.

2. When involved in speech acts, the desire is to know the information communicated did not infringe upon the rights of another, but also that conditions of equality for all are protected.

B. The Teleology philosophy has a focus on the end result.
   1. An ethical communicator grounded in a teleological philosophy is governed by the best possible outcome from their choices of speech acts.
   2. The communicator will weigh the different outcomes and decide what will be the best of all possibilities and govern their speech act accordingly.
C. Deontological philosophy suggests that the ethical speaker will do what their individual commitment to a faith or guiding principles will support and will not deviate.
   1. The ethical speaker has pledged to uphold certain principles and the speech act should be governed by those principles.
   2. Ideally, both parties in the communiqué would be guided by the same principles.

Name: _____ Section: _____ Date: _____

10.1 Ethics and Self-reflection

In the space provided, define ethics in your own terms. Discuss how you came to define ethics this way. Where did you learn your values, morals, and beliefs? Analyze how your definition of ethics influences the choices you make and the life you lead. How has your past influenced the choices you make in the present?

_____

_____

_____

_____

_____

_____

_____

_____

_____

_____

_____

_____

_____

_____

_____

_____

10.2 Theoretical Ethics

After reading the section about ethical communication theories in Chapter 10, discuss when you think each of the three theories would be useful in a speech setting. Additionally, research different examples of speeches and find one example for each speech theory.

	Virtue Ethics
Useful when…	
Useful when…	
Example of Use	
	Taoist Ethics
Useful when…	
Useful when…	
Example of Use	
	Dialogic Ethics
Useful when…	
Useful when…	
Example of Use	

Name: _____ Section: _____ Date: _____

10.3 What Would You Do?

Read the scenario provided. Determine what would you do if you were in that situation.

I clicked on the discussion board prompt eager to get the work out of my way so I could start my weekend earlier. The prompt read:

In your own words, what is a visual aid? What makes a good visual aid? What makes a bad visual aid? Why are visual aids important to public speaking?

"Seems simple enough," I thought to myself. Before posting my own response, I decided to check out what my classmates had posted. That is when I noticed something wasn't right. That girl surely did not write that. Her previous postings always had grammar mistakes and her English was choppy. This is perfect grammar and no spelling mistakes. My curiosity got the best of me so I cut and pasted a few of the lines my classmate wrote and Googled them. At least 50 websites popped up with those exact same lines. Do I email the instructor? Do I even bring it to the instructor's attention? Is it my place to say anything? After all, it is only a discussion board for my communication class. Is plagiarizing bad, whether it is big or small?

_____

_____

_____

_____

_____

_____

_____

10.4 Ethics Gone Wrong

Has there been a time when your individual ethics have failed you? A time when you broke your own code of ethics? Describe a scenario where your application of ethics has been misguided, and a time when you broke your ethical code. How did these experiences shape future dealings with ethical considerations?

Misguided Ethics:

_____

_____

_____

_____

_____

_____

Broken Ethics:

_____

_____

_____

_____

_____

_____

10.5 Individual versus Collective

Many people face situations where their ethical codes do not match those of a group that they are involved in (at least not to the letter). One example of this is that the Catholic church does not support the use of birth control, yet many Catholics practice safe sex. Think about your own group affiliations–what are the ethics espoused by the group? Do they agree or disagree with your own? How does that impact your communication within the group?

Group Ethics	Personal Ethics	Communication with Group

10.6 Ethical Audit

After reading the story about Armstrong Williams in the ethical audit section of Chapter 10, perform an ethical audit with regard to the story. How does this story make you feel? Was Williams' behavior ethical in your opinion? Answer the following questions:

1. Is it right? _____

_____

2. Is it fair? _____

_____

3. Is it restrictive or deceptive to others? _____

_____

4. Who does it affect? _____

_____

5. Who does it serve? _____

_____

6. Is it something one might become ashamed of when it comes to light? _____

_____

7. Would I have behaved in a similar fashion? Why or why not? _____

_____

Name: _____ Section: _____ Date: _____

Test Yourself

Match these vocabulary terms with the descriptions that best define them.

1. _____ Ethics

a. Appraisal of situations that challenge morality

2. _____ Egalitarianism

b. Goal of social equity, fairness and justice

3. _____ Moral Absolute

c. Promoting concept of natural balance

4. _____ Moral Relativism

d. Focuses on commitment to guiding principles

5. _____ Ethical Audit

e. Consider that there are other ethical systems that others choose and their choices are respected

6. _____ Virtue Ethics

f. Moral principles for living and making decisions

7. _____ Taoist Ethics

g. Focuses on the end result

8. _____ Dialogic Ethics

h. Avoiding rhetorical manipulation and objectification

9. _____ Teleology Philosophy

i. Determines right and wrong from their perceived absolute truths

10. _____ Deontological Philosophy

j. Unity of facts and reason

chapter Eleven

Topic Purpose Thesis: The Building Blocks

Chapter Outline

Practice your outlining skills by filling in the blank spaces.

I. Selecting a Topic
   A. "Getting a topic" is the most difficult part of a speech assignment.
      1. Most of us feel challenged and somewhat threatened by a speaking assignment, and generally, we wish that we had greater resources at hand.
      2. If we take time to assess our accumulation of knowledge about ourselves and our ideas, we will readily recognize those subjects on which we are prepared to speak and those subjects for which additional preparation will be necessary.
   B. There is a significant difference between being prepared to speak on a topic and becoming prepared to speak on it.
      1. This is the difference between general preparation and specific preparation for speaking.
      2. The speaker's prior experience, reading, and deliberation about a topic constitutes that speakers general preparation for speaking on that topic.
      3. Once the subject is in mind, the additional research, organization, planning, and practice for the event make up the specific preparation.
II. Research
   A. Newspaper columns, magazine articles, web sites, lecture notes (all with citations listing the source, author, and date) should be filed systematically for future reference.
   B. A successful presentation is usually judged by its content. Its content is developed based on the research.
   C. Notes from "I've Got to Do a Research Paper for This Class"
      1.
      2.
      3.
      4.
      5.

6.

7.

8.

9.

10.

11.

12.

III. What Is My Purpose?

    A. When you are giving a speech, it is your responsibility to determine the general purpose of the speech.

        1. Most speeches fall under one of three different purposes: to entertain, to inform, or to persuade.

        2. It is easy to determine the purpose of your speech by asking questions like:

            a. What do I want my audience to know?

            b. What do I want my audience to do?

            c. How is the best way to achieve what I want from my audience?

            d. Is what I want to achieve feasible?

        3. The way that you answer those questions determines the general purpose of your speech.

        4. General purpose statements should be stated in a single infinitive phrase: to inform, to persuade, to entertain.

            a. If your purpose is to entertain the audience, you are generally the person that inspires the audience.

            b. A speaker that informs is responsible for enlightening the audience and providing them with information that they probably did not already know.

            c. Persuasive speeches seek some type of behavioral or attitudinal modification. Your general purpose is to sway the audience toward your perspective on the facts, values, or policies.

    B. The first step in developing any speech is to know your purpose.

    C. A specific purpose is a general purpose plus one main aspect of your topic.

        1. The specific purpose narrows your topic so that you can focus on accomplishing one specific goal.

        2. The specific purpose of any speech should be stated concisely and should clearly and specifically state what the speaker wants to achieve.

        3. It should also be stated in infinitive form.

        4. It should address one main idea and should focus your presentation

    D. Is my purpose relevant to my audience?

        1.

        2.

    E. Have I stated my purpose in clear and concise language?

        1.

        2.

F. Will I be able to achieve this purpose?
1.
2.

IV. Thesis Statement/Preview
A. The thesis statement/preview tells exactly what you plan to do in the speech.
B. It essentially lays out your main idea and provides a general idea of the evidence that you will use to support that idea.
C. In one declarative statement, you should state your thesis/preview for your speech.

Name: _____   Section: _____ Date: _____

11.1 Brainstorm for Topics

Think about what types of speeches interest you. What are you passionate about? What do you think you could present to your audience in an effective way? Using the space below, brainstorm (or free-associate) possible topics for speeches.

11.2 Trusting Online Resources[1]

For each of the following web sites answer these questions.

1. Does the design and overall "look and feel" of the Web site indicate a professional effort? _____

2. Who is the author of this Web site? _____

3. Is this Web site funded by the author, advertisements, donations, or a combination thereof? _____

4. When was this Web site last updated or what is the most recent date you see? _____

_____

5. Does the Web site cite any sources it used or does it have a webliography? _____

_____

6. Does the Web site represent a specific cause, issue, or bias? _____

7. Can you find some of the information featured in this Web site on a different one?

_____

8. Would you trust this Web site and use it as a source for information? _____

www.bigredhair.com/boilerplate

Meet the world's first Victorian era robot.

1. Y / N   2. _____   3. _____   4._____

5. Y / N   6. Y / N   7. Y / N   8. Y / N

www.dumblaws.com

Did you know that in North Carolina it is illegal to plow a cotton field with an elephant?

1. Y / N   2. _____   3. _____   4._____

5. Y / N   6. Y / N   7. Y / N   8. Y / N

www.snopes.com

Did the Sesame Street Muppet Bert really support Bin Laden?

1. Y / N   2. _____   3. _____   4._____

5. Y / N   6. Y / N   7. Y / N   8. Y / N

---
[1] Contributed by S. Cashman.

Name: _____ Section: _____ Date: _____

www.clubbo.com

From Indonesian punk rock to Christian heavy metal, this site has it all. Check out the artist profiles.

   1. Y / N   2. _____   3. _____   4._____

   5. Y / N   6. Y / N   7. Y / N   8. Y / N

www.thedogisland.com

Does your dog need to unwind? Send them to Dog Island, the most impressive canine getaway out there.

   1. Y / N   2. _____   3. _____   4._____

   5. Y / N   6. Y / N   7. Y / N   8. Y / N

www.theonion.com

America's finest news source.

   1. Y / N   2. _____   3. _____   4._____

   5. Y / N   6. Y / N   7. Y / N   8. Y / N

11.3 Scavenger Hunt: Library Style

Visit your school's library to find answers to the following questions.

1. On which floor, can you find a book about the Spanish Armada? _____

   _____

2. How many copies of To Kill A Mockingbird does your library carry? _____

   _____

3. Write the names of all the journals that your library carries that contain the phrase "Journal of". _____

   _____

4. How many different sets of encyclopedias are in the reference section? _____

   _____

5. How many librarians sit at the reference desk during peak hours? _____

   _____

6. What are the libraries hours? _____

   _____

7. How long can an undergraduate check out a book? How long can a graduate student check out a book? _____

   _____

8. What is the call number for a book about Dorothy Dandridge? Title? Author?

   _____

9. How many copy machines are in the library? _____

   _____

10. How are books categorized in the library? _____

Name: _____ *Section:* _____ *Date:* _____

11.4 Collecting Information

Read the section titled "Pass the Collection Plate" in Chapter 11. Using the topics you came up with in Activity 11.1 (Brainstorming), think of sources for information about these topics. The sources may be books and articles, as well as Web sites. Also try to think of sources that are personal to you, such as interviews, personal experiences, and family stories. Make a list of at least five sources for a minimum of two topics.

Topic One _____

Sources:

1.

2.

3.

4.

5.

Topic Two _____

Sources:

1.

2.

3.

4.

5.

11.5 Einstein or DaVinci

According to Dr. Whitley, paper writing is both an art and a science. Using your brainstorming (Activity 11.1) topics, begin to think about your strengths and weaknesses for the topics you have selected. Can you write a creative, intellectually stimulating (art) paper on this topic, or are you more focused on the technical writing and research aspects (science) of the paper? The ultimate goal is to do both. List your strengths and weaknesses for each aspect of paper-writing below, and think about ways you can improve each.

Art

Strengths	Weaknesses	Improvements

Science

Strengths	Weaknesses	Improvements

Name: _____ *Section:* _____ *Date:* _____

11.6 Goals and Thesis

Using the space below, write out goal and thesis statements for a minimum of two speech topics. Be creative, be concise, and be specific.

Topic One

General Goal:

Specific Goal:

Thesis Statement:

Topic Two

General Goal:

Specific Goal:

Thesis Statement:

Name: _____ *Section:* _____ *Date:* _____

Test Yourself

Match these vocabulary terms with the descriptions that best define them.

1. _____ Topic   a. Inspiring the audience

2. _____ Research   b. What you will discuss in speech

3. _____ Thesis Statement   c. Calling the audience to action

4. _____ To Entertain   d. General purpose plus one main aspect of topic

5. _____ To Inform   e. Gathering information about topic

6. _____ To Persuade   f. Main focus of presentation

7. _____ Specific Purpose   g. Passing along factual information

8. _____ Preview   h. What you plan to do in the speech

chapter Twelve

Audience Analysis: "Don't Talk to Strangers"

Chapter Outline

Practice your outlining skills by filling in the blank spaces.

I. Be aware of and sensitive to the major components of the speech process.
   A. Understanding How the Self Functions in the Public Speaking Event
      1. Try to formulate a clear concept of yourself *as a speaker.*
      2. Try to see yourself *as others see you* in the act of speaking.
      3. As a first step, you should endeavor to *systematically* make a careful, objective analysis of your feelings and behaviors in a number of speech communication *situations.*
   B. Understanding the "Other" in the Public Speaking Event
      1. The "Others" in the speech communication context will comprise your listeners-your audience.
      2. The analysis of audiences begins and is inextricably interwoven with the history of rhetorical theory.
      3. Aristotle, who also devoted much attention to audience analysis, discusses in the *Rhetoric* what an audience is likely to consider good.
         a. Aristotle touches upon several human emotions-anger, fear, love, shame, and pity.
         b. Aristotle examines the effects produced by the various emotions on listeners and the factors which create those effects.
   C. "What Is Their Motivation Here?"
      1. The analysis of audience behavior is also a central concern in contemporary research in communication.
         a.
         b.
      2. When preparing to speak with any audience, you should try to assess the dominant values and motives which will be operative in the audience at the time of the speaking event.

     3. The audience analysis procedure can assist you in two important ways.

        a. First, it will reveal to you the nature of the audience you will face; you will become more aware of the types of personalities represented among your listeners.

        b. Second, by discovering the present thought position (and nature) of your audience, you can more knowledgeably determine the directions and emphases your speaking must take in order to move the thinking of that audience to the desired position on the subject.

     4. In analyzing an audience, seek out all of the information you can about the others who are or will be in the communication setting.

II. The Feedback Principle

  A. What can be done to gain and maintain the participation of the listening audience?

     1. In planning for a speech act you must think in terms of your listeners and must plan with them in mind.

     2. In this preplanning, you will find that the principle of feedback functions in at least two very useful ways.

        a. It enables you to allow for "feedforward."

        b. It enables you to adjust more readily and effectively to feedback from your listeners during the actual communication of your message.

  B. Adjusting to Feedback from Your Audience

     1. This step involves an on the spot, face-to-face problem which you can detect and solve only with your actual audience before you.

     2. You must correctly interpret your audience members' responses as you are speaking and you must adapt to that response very quickly.

     3. The requisite skill is adaptive readiness.

     4. One of the key differences between planning for feedforward and adjusting to feedback is that in the former you are, in effect, predicting probabilities but in the latter you are facing immediate activities.

        a.

        b.

  C. Audience Rapport

     1. Good rapport, the empathy that one human being has for another, and the relationship it seeks to identify should be one of your guiding goals as you plan and incorporate feedforward.

     2.

  D. Reacting to Absence of Feedback

     1. The inability respond to others in real life situations is a form of mental illness. and under so-called "normal" day-to-day conditions, failure to provide and receive feedback can do inestimable harm.

     2.

  E. Overreacting to Feedback

     1.

     2.

     3.

F. Language Adaptation

    1.

    2.

    3.

G. Stasis

    1.

    2.

    3.

III. Understanding the Context of the Impending Communication

    A. You must make yourself aware of the specific speaking situation or setting, the particular elements which will be multidimensionally, multidirectionally, and simultaneously operant within it and upon the interactants because:

        1. The specific context constraints and directs your choices of materials and approaches.

        2. The specific context helps you as the speaker to determine what is expected of you.

        3. The specific context helps you to define what is desired of the speaker.

        4. The specific context bears importantly upon what is required of the speaker.

        5. The context strongly influences the outcomes of the communication act.

    B. Context has both physical and psychological dimensions.

        1. Those dimensions are significantly influenced by certain social, temporal, and cultural factors.

        2. They are the contemporaneous, causative, and circumstantial influences which bear upon an impeding communication event.

    C. Contemporaneous Influences

        1.

        2.

    D. Causative Influences

        1.

        2.

    E. Circumstantial Influences

        1.

        2.

Name: _____ *Section:* _____ *Date:* _____

12.1 Know Your Audience

Using the grid below, analyze your fellow classmates so that you will have a better understanding of what speech topics they would be interested in hearing.

Median Age	
Median Education Level	
Race	
Religion	
Interests	
History	

12.2 Slang and Lingo

Based on your audience analysis from Activity 12.1, what type of language would you use in your presentation to classmates? What if your audience was composed of different members? Would you alter your language? How so? Why is language adaptation important when giving speeches?

_____

_____

_____

_____

_____

_____

_____

_____

_____

_____

_____

_____

_____

_____

_____

Name: _____ *Section:* _____ *Date:* _____

12.3 Language and Music

Pick three songs from three different genres of music. Listen to the song. Listen to the song again while reading the lyrics. Fill in the chart listing the song's title and examples of figurative language. Explain in the last column what you think the language means.

Song (Title and Artist)	Example of Figurative Language	Your interpretation

12.4 Anxiety Reduction

Make a list of speaking situations that cause you anxiety. Rank them from highest anxiety to lowest anxiety. Next, write down steps to take that will help you reduce anxiety for each given scenario.

Rank	Scenario	Steps to Reduce Anxiety

Chapter Two

Name: _____ Section: _____ Date: _____

12.5 You as the Speaker

Think about who you are. How do you see yourself? How do others see you? In what ways are these similar or different viewpoints? When speaking, you want to gain the respect and trust of your audience quickly. To do this, you should know yourself, as well as how others perceive you. Think about your speech topic, and make a list of the ways in which you see yourself as a credible speaker on this topic. Then make a list of how you are going to demonstrate this credibility to your audience.

I am credible because:

1.

2.

3.

4.

5.

I will demonstrate my credibility to the audience by:

1.

2.

3.

4.

5.

12.6 Audience Motivation and Bias

After you have completed your audience analysis, you will have a better understanding of who "they" are. Think about what is motivating them to listen to and understand your speech. What biases might the audience members have regarding your speech topic? How will you, as a speaker, overcome these biases in your speech?

What is motivating your audience?

1.

2.

3.

4.

What biases does your audience have regarding your topic?

1.

2.

3.

4.

How will you overcome these biases in your speech?

1.

2.

3.

4.

Name: _____ Section: _____ Date: _____

Test Yourself

Match these vocabulary terms with the descriptions that best define them.

1. _____ Speaking Anxiety

2. _____ Audience Analysis

3. _____ Contemporaneous Influences

4. _____ Causative Influences

5. _____ Circumstantial Influences

6. _____ Rapport

7. _____ Language Adaptation

8. _____ Stasis

a. Time and timing

b. Empathy one person feels for another

c. Considering audience demographics

d. Audience expectations

e. Changing speaking style to meet audience needs

f. Apprehension when speaking in public

g. Status of the case

h. Impetuses or forces

chapter Thirteen

Making Informative Speaking Sound Conversational

Chapter Outline

Practice your outlining skills by filling in the blank spaces.

I. There are several issues that you must attend to in order to become more effective in your informational presentations.

   A. Effective informational presenters perform sound audience analysis.

      1. Audience analysis is when the speaker gathers information on the demographics of your audience.

         a. Information includes the age of your audience members, their sex, their race, the psychological makeup of your audience.

         b. Psychological makeup includes knowing what is meaningful to them, knowing their attitude toward your topic, knowing what they know about your topic, and finally, knowing what they think about you.

      2. Conducting an audience analysis also includes knowing the context of the public speaking engagement. Speakers should know where the presentation is being held, know about the room, and know why the event is taking place.

      3. In general, what you learn from the audience analysis is going to influence how you package or organize your message. It will inform the language that you use.

      4. Audience analysis even influences our appearance.

   B. Develop a strong introduction, include strong evidence and transitions in a well-organized body. Conclude presentations by reviewing main points and leaving the audience with a memorable final thought.

II. Parts of the Speech

   A. Introductions should address five specific areas. It should gain the attention of the audience; tell the audience why they should listen, establish your credibility, tell what and how you plan to accomplish what you came to do.

      1. First, gain the audience's attention.

      2. Next, provide motivation or a reason to listen.

3. Third, establish your credibility by explaining how you became knowledgeable about what you are discussing.

   a. Establish your credibility by letting the audience know how you know.

   b. The central theme or thesis of your discussion is the concise statement that explains what you are going to be discussing.

4. Finally, let the audience know what evidence you have to support your claim. This is called previewing.

B. In the body of the speech, be conservative in the number of main points that you include in your speech.

   1. Audiences can comfortably handle three to five main points.

   2. Use transitions between your main points.

      a. Transitions are guides for your audience; they let the audience know where the speaker is going and where the speaker has been.

      b. Transitions can be verbal or nonverbal. Verbal transitions are words or sentences that connect ideas and the parts of your speech. Nonverbal transitions are physical behaviors that signal to your audience that you are introducing new points or that you are moving on from the present point.

C. Your conclusion is the last thing that your friend, Audience, is going to hear from you.

   1. Speakers reinforce their purpose and their main points by reviewing them for their audience.

   2. Speakers leave the audience wanting more. Give your audience something to think about. Provide them with a final emotive, thought-provoking saying, i.e., a memorable final thought. Your audience should not leave your presentation wondering what it was about.

III. There are five forms of evidence that we usually use to support public presentations: statistics, examples, comparisons, quotes/expert testimony, and visual aids.

A. Statistics are numbers that summarize or expand the view of the problem. Make sure your statistics are current. In an effort to keep your presentation flowing, you should round numbers off during your delivery.

B. Examples can be quick references, detailed examples, hypothetical examples, stories or extended examples, which include lots of detail.

C. Comparisons state associations between two things that are similar in important respects. Remember, similes and metaphors are great ways to compare like and unlike items.

D. Quotes or expert testimony are quotations and/or expressions made by individuals whom the audience respects, such as an expert who is qualified to speak on the specific issue.

E. Visual aids reinforce your verbal message. Please spare your audience; keep your visual aids simple, clear, clean, and uncluttered.

IV. There are several ways to organize presentations.

A. Chronological method allows you to organize your speech based on time relationships. You may consider talking about events in the order in which they have occurred.

B. Topical method allows you to organize your speech into several categories or areas of focus. As the label implies, your speech may progress from subtopic to subtopic.

C. Comparative method allows you to organize your speech by comparing two or more situations so that you can emphasize their differences and similarities.

D. Problem-Solution method allows you to organize your speech into a discussion of a problem and solution.

E. Cause-Effect and Effect-Cause allows you to organize your speech so that you can argue that one situation is directly caused by another.

V. Seeing and Hearing the Speech

A. Gestures

1. A gesture is "a movement of the body or limbs that expresses or emphasizes an idea."

2. Gestures are powerful. They create a bond between you and the audience.

3. Gestures should not draw attention to themselves, but to the correlating message you are trying to emphasize.

B. Controlling the One Big Nerve

1. Find a place to direct your nervous energy. You might find that you are more comfortable walking from one side of the lectern to the other side at a controlled pace.

2. Always remember to take deep breaths. Deep breathing works wonders for the nerves. Don't pant, just breathe deeply.

C. Freedom Exercise

1. Find a quiet place, where you feel free from the anxiousness caused by daily life. As you prepare to free your mind, you may find that soft music will help in this relaxation process. Let's get started.

D. Again, Don't Imitate

1. Find your own delivery style.

2. Appear as natural as possible.

3. Delivery style should be appropriate to the context of the speech.

E. Country Grammar Won't Work Here

1. Poor grammar is an audience turnoff.

2. Most people perceive poor grammar as a sign of ignorance and/or lack of education.

F. Vocalized Pauses

1. Many speakers use some type of silence fillers when they speak. Examples are Ah, uh, mm, nata mean (you know what I mean) simply fill the silent moments.

Name: _____ Section: _____ Date: _____

13.1 Process Speeches and the Food Network

Have you ever noticed how cooking preparation shows and home improvement shows demonstrate how to complete a meal or a project? Your assignment is to watch a food preparation show i.e., *Thirty Minute Meals, In the Kitchen with Bobby Flay, Food Rescue 911, How to Boil Water, Emeril Live*. Write down the various steps the chef uses to prepare one of the meals. Next, write an introduction that you could use to teach others what you learn.

Steps

1.

2.

3.

4.

5.

6.

Introduction

_____

_____

_____

_____

_____

_____

13.2 Informative Speech and Community Activist

When giving an informative speech, you have the task of presenting new information to your audience. One of the great things about cities like Greensboro, NC; Selma, AL; and Montgomery, AL is their contribution to the Civil Rights movement.

You recently learned that you have to give an informative speech about a person who was directly involved in the Civil Rights movement. The catch is that you have to find new information. Pick one of the following individuals and research information to share with your class that you believe could be included in an informative speech.

- Ralph Abernathy

- Robert F. Kennedy

- President Lyndon Johnson

- Ezell Blair, Jr.

- David Richmond

- Joseph McNeil

- Franklin McCain

- Virginia Foster Durr

- Thurgood Marshall

- Coretta Scott King

- Fredrick Douglas

Name: _____ *Section:* _____ *Date:* _____

13.3 Watching Others Inform

Reflect on an individual, whether a teacher, a guest speaker, a member of a clergy, a city leader, whom you feel is a good communicator. Discuss specific techniques the individual uses to make their speech/discussion/lectures clear, interesting, and memorable. _____

_____

_____

_____

_____

Now, if you had the opportunity to master one of their public speaking abilities, what would it be? Why? _____

_____

_____

_____

_____

Given what you know about informative speaking, how would you classify their informative speech? If you had the chance to give the same informative speech, what would you do differently? _____

_____

_____

_____

_____

_____

13.4 Delivery Style

Who do you admire as a public speaker? What is their delivery style when speaking? What traits can you use in your own delivery style? Remember, just because it works for them does not mean it will work for you. Combine traits from different individuals that you feel comfortable adapting into your own delivery style.

Public Speaker	Admirable Speaking Traits

Name: _____ *Section:* _____ *Date:* _____

13.5 Organizational Methods

Certain speeches are more appropriate for each organizational method. List an example of a speech topic that is best suited for each of the organizational methods listed below.

Chronological Method: _____

_____

Topical Method: _____

_____

Comparative Method: _____

_____

Problem-Solution Method: _____

_____

Cause-Effect Method: _____

_____

Effect-Cause Method: _____

_____

13.6 Conclusions

Design a conclusion for an informative speech (you may use the one in Activity 13.1, for example). Remember; be sure to include a statement that reflects on the information you have given throughout your speech, as well as a "closing statement." Your closing statement should be the last thing you want your audience to remember about you and your speech topic.

Concluding Remarks

_____

_____

_____

_____

_____

_____

_____

_____

_____

_____

Name: _____ Section: _____ Date: _____

Test Yourself

Match these vocabulary terms with the descriptions that best define them.

1. _____ Audience Analysis

2. _____ Statistics

3. _____ Examples

4. _____ Comparisons

5. _____ Expert Testimony

6. _____ Visual Aids

7. _____ Chronological Method

8. _____ Topical Method

9. _____ Comparative Method

10 _____ Problem-Solution Method

a. Associations between things that are similar in important respects

b. Organized on time relationships

c. Organized by situation and outcome

d. Numbers that summarize/expand view of the problem

e. Items that reinforce messages

f. Organized by comparison

g. Gathering demographic information about your listeners

h. Statements by knowledgeable/respected people

i. Organized by areas of focus

j. Quick references, detailed examples, hypothetical examples, stories or extended examples, which include lots of detail

chapter Fourteen

Persuasive Presentations: Using What You've Got to Get What You Want

Chapter Outline

Practice your outlining skills by filling in the blank spaces.

I. Rhetoric
   A. Rhetoric is the fundamental way people use language to accomplish their ends.
   B. Rhetoric and persuasion are very similar.
      1. The relationship is so intimate that they are often considered as one.
      2. Rhetoric, however, has its own set of theories, just as persuasion has its own.
   C. Rhetoric was developed by a group of orators, educators, and advocates called Sophists.
      1. Sophists is derived from the Greek word "sophos," meaning wise or skilled.
      2. The title "Sophistes" (pl. *Sophistae*) carried with it something of the modern meaning of professor-an authority, an expert, a teacher.
   D. Plato
      1.
      2.
   E. Aristotle
      1.
      2.
   F. Rhetoric offers a systematic, philosophical approach to giving speeches.
      1. Forensic
         a.
         b.
      2. Epideictic
         a.
         b.

    3. Deliberative

       a.

       b.

II. Rhetoric and the Everyday Speech

   A. Think of rhetoric in terms of developing a speech.

      1.

      2.

   B. We use rhetoric to transmit emotions and thoughts through a system of symbols so that we can influence other people's decisions or actions.

      1.

      2.

III. How does rhetorical discourse differ from other types of communication?

   A. Rhetoric is planned.

      1.

      2.

      3.

   B. Rhetoric is adapted to an audience.

IV. Social Functions of Rhetoric

   A. Rhetoric tests ideas.

      1.

      2.

   B. Rhetoric assists advocacy.

      1.

      2.

      3.

   C. Rhetoric discovers facts.

      1.

      2.

   D. Rhetoric builds community.

      1.

      2.

       a.

       b.

       c.

V. Developing Persuasive Presentations

   A. Persuasion is the process of preparing and presenting, verbal and nonverbal messages with the purpose of evaluating, sustaining, or altering the reality of an audience.

   B. Generally, persuasive presentations aim to either convince or to motivate.

      1.

      2.

C. Usually, persuasive presentations arise out of a speaker's desire to question facts, values, or policies.

    1.

    2.

    3.

D. In any persuasive speech, you want some type of action, whether it be passive agreement or vigorous activity.

    1.

    2.

    3.

VI. Persuasive Presentations in Business

A. Definition of Persuasive Presentation

B.

C. Stasis

D. Ethos and the Persuasive Speaker

    1. The ethical appeal of a speaker mainly reflects his character and how the audience perceives his character.

    2.

E. Logos

    1. Logos usually refers to the orderly thinking of sequencing and relating one thought or idea to another.

    2. A claim is a statement or declaration that we want others to accept; evidence is support for your claim, the facts that make your argument believable.

    3.

    4.

    5. Evidence for persuasive presentations can take the form of statistics, examples, comparisons, quotes or expert testimony, and visual aids.

VII. Putting Together a Persuasive Presentation

A. Topical/Claim Pattern

    1.

    2.

    3.

B. Cause/Effect/Solution or Action Pattern

    1.

    2.

    3.

C. Problem/Solution/Benefit or Action Pattern

    1.

    2.

    3.

D. Comparative Advantages Pattern

    1.

    2.

    3.

E. Monroe's Motivated Sequence

    1.

    2.

    3.

    4.

    5.

Name: _____ *Section:* _____ *Date:* _____

14.1 Persuasive Speaking and Literature

Read the following excerpt from Harper Lee's novel, *To Kill a Mockingbird.* After reading the excerpt, answer the following questions.

Finch: To begin with, this case should never have come to trial. The State has not produced one iota of medical evidence that the crime Tom Robinson is charged with ever took place. It has relied instead upon the testimony of two witnesses whose evidence has not only been called into serious question on cross examination, but has been flatly contradicted by the defendant. Now there is circumstantial evidence to indicate that Mayella Ewell was beaten, savagely, by someone who led, almost exclusively, with his left [hand]. And Tom Robinson now sits before you, having taken "The Oath" with the only good hand he possesses-his right.

I have nothing but pity in my heart for the Chief Witness for the State. She is the victim of cruel poverty and ignorance. But my pity does not extend so far as to her putting a man's life at stake, which she has done in an effort to get rid of her own guilt. Now I say "guilt," gentlemen, because it was guilt that motivated her. She's committed no crime. She's merely broken a rigid and time-honored code of our society, a code so severe that whoever breaks it is hounded from our midst as unfit to live with. She must destroy the evidence of her offense. But, what was the evidence of her offense? Tom Robinson, a human being. She must put Tom Robinson away from her. Tom Robison was to her a daily reminder of what she did. Now what did she do? She tempted a Negro. She was white and she tempted a Negro. She did something that in our society is unspeakable: She kissed a black man. Not an old uncle, but a strong, young Negro man. No code mattered to her before she broke it, but it came crashing down on her afterwards.

The witnesses for the State, with the exception of the sheriff of Lincoln county, have presented themselves to you gentlemen-to this Court-in the cynical confidence that their testimony would not be doubted; confident that you gentlemen would go along with them on the assumption, the evil assumption, that all Negroes lie; all Negroes are basically immoral beings; all Negro men are not to be trusted around our women-an assumption that one associates with minds of their caliber, and which is in itself, gentlemen, a lie-which I do not need to point out to you.

And so, a quiet, humble, respectable Negro, who has had the unmitigated temerity to feel sorry for a white woman, has had to put his word against two white peoples. The defendant is not guilty. But somebody in this courtroom is.

Now, gentlemen, in this country our courts are the great levelers. In our courts, all men are created equal. I'm no idealist to believe firmly in the integrity of our courts and of our jury system. That's no ideal to me. That is a living, working reality! Now I am confident that you gentlemen will review, without passion, the evidence that you have heard, come to a decision, and restore this man to his family. In the name of God, do your duty. In the name of God, believe Tom Robinson.

1. What pattern of persuasive speaking did Atticus use in his closing arguments?

2. How would you define the demographic of Atticus' audience?

3. How did Atticus use ethos, logos, and pathos?

4. If you were on the jury, would you have voted guilty or not guilty during jury deliberations? Why or why not?

5. What forms of evidence did Atticus summarize?

6. In your opinion, was this closing argument an effective persuasive speech?

Name: _____ *Section:* _____ *Date:* _____

14.2 Persuasion and Commercials

During the 2005 Superbowl between the New England Patriots and Philadelphia Eagles, a thirty-second commercial spot cost 2.4 million dollars. The 2005 Superbowl was seen by over 80 million people.

Part One

Describe your favorite commercial and examine what ways the commercial uses appeal to try and persuade the audience to purchase their product. (Use an additional sheet of paper if necessary.)

_____

_____

_____

_____

_____

_____

Part Two

With two or three other individuals, discuss the following questions and report your findings back to the class.

1. What appeals do commercials use to draw in consumers?

2. What commercials do you believe to be the most memorable?

3. Are commercials an effective example of persuasive appeal?

4. What is an example of an ineffective commercial? Why do you consider this commercial ineffective?

14.3 Monroe's Motivated Sequence and Current Events

Pick a "hot topic." One that is an event or issue currently being debated on the news or in the newspaper. Using Monroe's Motivated Sequence, examine how you would present a persuasive speech on this topic.

Action: _____

_____

_____

Need: _____

_____

_____

Satisfaction _____

_____

_____

Visualization: _____

_____

_____

Action: _____

_____

_____

Name: _____ *Section:* _____ *Date:* _____

14.4 Aristotle's System of Rhetoric

Chapter 14 offers you one example of each type of speech from Aristotle's system of rhetoric. On your own, offer at least two more examples of speeches you have witnessed or know about for each type of speech system. Additionally, think of a speech you could give that would align itself with each of the categories.

	Forensic
Example One	
Example Two	
Your Speech Idea	
	Epideictic
Example One	
Example Two	
Your Speech Idea	
	Deliberative
Example One	
Example Two	
Your Speech Idea	

14.5 Social Functions

Select a speech topic for a persuasive speech. How will you adapt your speech to meet Herrick's social functions of rhetoric discussed in Chapter 14?

Speech Topic

How will my speech *test ideas* about popular thought regarding the subject? _____

_____

How will my speech *assist with advocacy* for the topic? _____

_____

How will I *discover facts* about my speech topic? _____

_____

How will my speech *shape knowledge* regarding the topic? _____

_____

How will my speech assist in *community building*? _____

_____

Name: _____ *Section:* _____ *Date:* _____

14.6 Fact, Value, or Policy

As you recently learned, persuasive speeches deal with questions of fact, value, and policy. Your thesis, or main idea, behind a persuasive speech should only concern one of these. Below, list examples of speech topics that will question facts, values, and policies.

	Questions of Fact
Example One	
Example Two	
Example Three	
	Questions of Value
Example One	
Example Two	
Example Three	
	Questions of Policy
Example One	
Example Two	
Example Three	

Name: _____ *Section:* _____ *Date:* _____

Test Yourself

Match these vocabulary terms with the descriptions that best define them.

1. _____ Rhetoric

2. _____ Forensic

3. _____ Epideictic

4. _____ Deliberative

5. _____ Rhetor

6. _____ Inventio

7. _____ Dispositio

8. _____ Elecutio

9. _____ Persuasion

10. _____ Claim

a. Public forum

b. Person who uses rhetoric

c. Delivery method

d. Purpose of evaluating, sustaining, or altering the reality of an audience

e. Using language to accomplish needs

f. Statement that we want others to accept

g. Ceremonial occasions

h. Invention

i. Oratory of the law courts

j. Arrangement

chapter Fifteen

Special Occasion Speeches

Chapter Outline

Practice your outlining skills by filling in the blank spaces.

I. Special Occasion Speeches
 A. The general purpose of a special occasion speech is to entertain.
 B. The specific purposes of these occasions may differ.
 C. There are several types of speeches that might be required at special occasions.
II. Welcome Speeches
 A. In the welcome speech, you welcome the audience to the event, state the purpose of the event and create enthusiasm about the event.
 B. What is the purpose of the public speaking event?
 1. It is important to know the exact purpose of the event.
 2. Be able to tell the audience that purpose.
 3. You also need to know the sponsors of the event and should acknowledge the leaders of the sponsoring group during your speech.
 4. Consider if the event is formal or informal.
 C. Who are the others/audience in the public speaking event?
 1. Address a specific audience that you are aware of and that you know.
 2. The type of event will inform your delivery decisions.
 D. What are my expectations of the audience?
 1. You want the audience to feel welcomed.
 2. You want the audience to pay attention to your message.
 E. Tips for Welcome Speeches
 1. Know the purpose of the event and share that during your presentation.
 2. Know the audience.
 3. Know the history and goals of the sponsoring group and link those goals back to the audience.
 4. Know the sponsors of the event and acknowledge the leadership of the sponsoring group.
 5. Enthuse the audience, most importantly, *welcome them!*

III. Introductory Speeches

    A. Introductory speeches create enthusiasm about the upcoming speaker.

    B. The general purpose is to enthuse.

    C. What is the purpose of the public speaking event?

        1. It is important to know the exact purpose of the event. It is just as important that you know your purpose.

            a. In an introductory speech, you are expected to build enthusiasm for the keynote speaker and his or her message.

            b. Your general purpose is to create enthusiasm about the person you are introducing.

    D. Who are the others/audience in the public speaking event?

        1.

        2.

    E. What are my expectations of the audience?

        1.

        2.

    F. Tips for Introductory Speeches

        1. Know the purpose of the event and why this speaker has been chosen as the keynote. If the speaker is chosen because of philanthropic contributions, you will want to relate primarily to his/her philanthropic achievements. On the other hand, if the speaker is chosen because of academic achievements, you will want to relate primarily to his/her academic ones.

        2. Know the audience. It is important that you find a way to link the speaker to the audience. What's the hook? Determine what your speaker and audience have in common and play on it. Your audience may desire to be like your speaker and are looking for inspiration. Inspire them.

        3. Know the person that you are introducing. Make sure you gather current, accurate information about the person you are introducing. If you are lucky, you can get a fact sheet about the person. If not, you need to make time to interview the person.

        4. Stress ideas that will make the person you are introducing seem as credible as possible. Remember; your general purpose is to create enthusiasm about the person that you are introducing.

        5. Don't read the boring chronological biography. Make it exciting.

        6. Have an interesting opening, a creative body, and end with a statement that begs for applause.

        7. Keep it brief. One to three minutes is usually enough. However, more accomplished keynote speakers may deserve a little longer introduction.

        8. Talk about the person you are introducing-not yourself. And make sure you don't play the person up so highly that they can never live up to their introduction. That is, *minimize the superfluous listing of glorifying adjectives.*

IV. Presentation Speeches

    A. In a presentation speech, you acknowledge the recipient of an award.

    B. The general purpose is to create enthusiasm about the award recipient. Tell what makes the recipient "so all that."

C. What is the purpose of the public speaking event?

    1.

    2.

D. Who are the others/audience in the public speaking event?

    1.

    2.

E. What are my expectations of the audience?

    1.

    2.

F. Tips for Presentation Speeches

    1. Know the purpose of the event and why this person is receiving the award. Focus on achievements that have led to the recognition or award.

    2. Know the audience. It is important that you find a way to link the recipient and the audience. What's the hook? Determine what your recipient and audience have in common and play on it.

    3. Strive to gain audience agreement. Stress ideas that will make the person you are introducing seem as credible as possible. You want to make the audience agree with you that this person should receive the award. Remember; your general purpose is to create enthusiasm about the person that is receiving the award.

    4. Don't read the boring chronological biography. Make it exciting.

    5. Have an interesting opening, a creative body, and end with a statement that begs for applause.

    6. Keep it brief. Presentation speeches can range from the "and the winner is" one-liners to five minutes. One to three minutes is usually enough.

V. Acceptance Speeches

A. In an acceptance speech, you give credit where credit is due-thank the appropriate people, tell what the award means to you, and how you got to where you are today.

B. Your general purpose in an acceptance speech is to inspire the audience.

C. What is the purpose of the public speaking event?

    1.

    2.

D. Who are the others/audience in the public speaking event?

    1.

    2.

E. What are my expectations of the audience?

    1.

    2.

F. Tips for Acceptance Speeches

    1. Know the purpose of the event and why you are receiving the award.

    2. Know the audience. It is important that you find a link between yourself and the audience. Find the hook? What do you have in common with the audience? Find that something and play on it. Inspire them.

3. Tell the audience what winning the award means to you.

4. Tell your "how I got over" story. Let the audience how you got to where you are now. Focus on the path that led to your receiving this recognition.

5. Don't read the boring chronological biography. Make it exciting. Tell us a story about that fifth grade teacher that was so inspirational in your getting to this place. The message here is to give life to the facts and faces to the names.

6. Have an interesting opening, a creative body, and end with a statement that begs for applause.

7. Stay within your time limit. Acceptance speeches can range from the "thank you" one-liners to an hour. I have heard Maya Angelou and John Hope Franklin give acceptance speeches that have a combined time of more than three hours. That's long. Just as you don't want to go over time, you definitely don't want to come up short either. Please ask the sponsors prior to the program to make sure of your time limitations.

VI. Master of Ceremony Speeches

    A. Definition of Master of Ceremonies (MC)

        1.

        2.

    B. The general purpose of the MC is to entertain.

        1. Entertain in this case means to create enthusiasm.

        2. You are to gain and retain the attention of the audience.

    C. You must know the role of each participant.

        1.

        2.

    D. You are the thread that weaves the entire program together.

        1.

        2.

    E. Tips for MC

        1. Know the purpose of the event.

        2. Know the audience.

        3. Know the entire program. You should not only know the program, but you should also convey specifics about the program to all the participants. Prior to the beginning of the program, let all the participants know where they are supposed to be and at what time. Make sure everyone participating in the program knows his or her responsibilities. For you to know all of this information, you should probably develop a script with an accompanying timeline and staging notes.

        4. Know the participants in the event. Please be able to pronounce the names of the people that you introduce. Don't say things like, "I hope I get this right, but is it pronounced Jah breeva?" Know how it is pronounced before you go in front of your audience.

        5. Don't just read the boring chronological agenda. Make it exciting. Keep the audience enthused throughout the program.

VII. Inspirational Speeches
    A. Definition of Inspirational Speeches
        1.
        2.
    B. After-Dinner Speeches
        1.
        2.
        3. What is the purpose of the public speaking event?
            a.
            b.
        4. Who are the others/audience in the public speaking event?
            a.
            b.
        5. What are my expectations of the audience?
            a.
            b.
        6. Tips for After-Dinner Speeches
            a. Know the purpose of the event and why you have been chosen to give this speech.
            b. Know the audience. Relate your topic to the audience. Use examples and illustrations that involve them or that relate to them.
            c. Don't read an after-dinner speech. You might read a poem, quote, etc., but do not read the speech. Make it exciting.
            d. Have an interesting opening, a creative body, and end with a statement that begs for applause. Find a novel way of treating the old.
            e. Know your time. Consult with the sponsors to determine the desired length of your presentation. You will also want to know whether the sponsors want you to speak prior to the meal or after. Groups generally stay away from having speakers talk during the meal. If you do find a group that is insistent upon you speaking at that time, try to dissuade them. It is incredibly difficult to speak during a meal. For the most part, people don't pay attention. Internal and external noise is too great.
    C. Commemorative Speeches
        1.
        2.
        3. What is the purpose of the public speaking event?
            a.
            b.
        4. Who are the others/audience in the public speaking event?
            a.
            b.

5. What are my expectations of the audience?

    a.

    b.

6. Tips for Commemorative Speeches

    a. Know the purpose of the event and why you are giving the commemorative address.

    b. Know the audience. Find and draw some parallels between the audience and the subject.

    c. Don't read lists. Make it exciting. Praise and celebrate.

    d. Have an interesting opening, a creative body, and end with a statement that begs for applause.

    e. Use vivid language that appeals to human emotion.

    f. Stay within your time limit. Contact the sponsoring group to determine your time constraints.

Name: _____ *Section:* _____ *Date:* _____

15.1 Speech of Introduction

It is a dream come true. Your favorite musician is coming to talk to one of the organizations you belong to and you have been given the task of introducing them. In the space provided, write a speech of introduction introducing your favorite musician.

_____

_____

_____

_____

_____

_____

_____

_____

_____

_____

_____

_____

_____

_____

15.2 Speech of Acceptance

Your department recently announced that you have been nominated for the department's annual scholarship. They will be hosting a luncheon where they will announce the winner. The catch is the winner is expected to say a few words. In the space provided, write a speech of acceptance.

_____

_____

_____

_____

_____

_____

_____

_____

_____

_____

_____

_____

_____

Name: _____ *Section:* _____ *Date:* _____

15.3 Dealing with Unexpected Disasters

Compare and contrast the speeches delivered by President Ronald Reagan and President George W. Bush after the Challenger and Columbia disasters. Answer the following questions in your analysis.

1. How do both presidents address the audience?

2. What do you notice about the language used?

3. How do the presidents personalize their speech?

4. What similarities do you notice in how they address each disaster?

5. How does religion influence the message?

6. Would the presidents dress matter in how the message is conveyed?

7. How did President Reagan and Bush partake in perspective taking?

8. Were the audience's religious beliefs/socioeconomic status/cultural beliefs and values/ and/or gender important for this speech? Why or why not?

9. What did you like about the address? What did you dislike about the address? If you were giving the speech, is there anything you would have done differently?

President Ronald Reagan
January 28, 1986
Remarks on the Challenger Disaster

Ladies and gentlemen, I'd planned to speak to you tonight to report on the state of the Union, but the events of earlier today have led me to change those plans. Today is a day for mourning and remembering. Nancy and I are pained to the core by the tragedy of the shuttle Challenger. We know we share this pain with all of the people of our country. This is truly a national loss.

Nineteen years ago, almost to the day, we lost three astronauts in a terrible accident on the ground. But we've never lost an astronaut in flight. We've never had a tragedy like this. And perhaps we've forgotten the courage it took for the crew of the shuttle. But they, the Challenger Seven, were aware of the dangers, but overcame them and did their jobs brilliantly. We mourn seven heroes: *Michael Smith, Dick Scobee, Judith Resnik, Ronald McNair, Ellison Onizuka, Gregory Jarvis,* and *Christa McAuliffe.* We mourn their loss as a nation together.

For the families of the seven, we cannot bear, as you do, the full impact of this tragedy. But we feel the loss, and we're thinking about you so very much. Your loved ones were daring and brave, and they had that special grace, that special spirit that says, "Give me a challenge, and I'll meet it with joy." They had a hunger to explore the universe and discover its truths. They wished to serve, and they did. They served all of us.

We've grown used to wonders in this century. It's hard to dazzle us. But for twenty-five years the United States space program has been doing just that. We've grown used to the idea of space, and, perhaps we forget that we've only just begun. We're still pioneers. They, the members of the Challenger crew, were pioneers.

And I want to say something to the schoolchildren of America who were watching the live coverage of the shuttle's take-off. I know it's hard to understand, but sometimes painful things like this happen. It's all part of the process of exploration and discovery. It's all part of taking a chance and expanding man's horizons. The future doesn't belong to the fainthearted; it belongs to the brave. The Challenger crew was pulling us into the future, and we'll continue to follow them.

I've always had great faith in and respect for our space program. And what happened today does nothing to diminish it. We don't hide our space program. We don't keep secrets and cover things up. We do it all up front and in public. That's the way freedom is, and we wouldn't change it for a minute.

We'll continue our quest in space. There will be more shuttle flights and more shuttle crews and, yes, more volunteers, more civilians, more teachers in space. Nothing ends here; our hopes and our journeys continue.

I want to add that I wish I could talk to every man and woman who works for NASA, or who worked on this mission and tell them: "Your dedication and professionalism have moved and impressed us for decades. And we know of your anguish. We share it."

There's a coincidence today. On this day three hundred and ninety years ago, the great explorer Sir Francis Drake died aboard ship off the coast of Panama. In his lifetime the great frontiers were the oceans, and a historian later said, "He lived by the sea, died on it, and was buried in it." Well, today, we can say of the Challenger crew: Their dedication was, like Drake's, complete.

The crew of the space shuttle Challenger honored us by the manner in which they lived their lives. We will never forget them, nor the last time we saw them, this morning, as they prepared for their journey and waved goodbye and "slipped the surly bonds of earth" to "touch the face of God."

Thank you.

Name: _____   *Section:* _____ *Date:* _____

President George W. Bush
February 1, 2003
Remarks on the Columbia Disaster

My fellow Americans, this day has brought terrible news and great sadness to our country. At nine o'clock this morning, mission control in Houston lost contact with our space shuttle Columbia. A short time later, debris was seen falling from the skies above Texas. The Columbia is lost; there are no survivors.

On board was a crew of seven: *Colonel Rick Husband; Lt. Colonel Michael Anderson; Commander Laurel Clark; Captain David Brown; Commander William McCool; Dr. Kalpana Chawla;* and *Ilan Ramon*, a *Colonel in the Israeli Air Force.* These men and women assumed great risk in the service to all humanity.

In an age when space flight has come to seem almost routine, it is easy to overlook the dangers of travel by rocket, and the difficulties of navigating the fierce outer atmosphere of the Earth. These astronauts knew the dangers, and they faced them willingly, knowing they had a high and noble purpose in life. Because of their courage, and daring, and idealism, we will miss them all the more.

All Americans today are thinking, as well, of the families of these men and women who have been given this sudden shock and grief. You're not alone. Our entire nation grieves with you. And those you loved will always have the respect and gratitude of this country. The cause in which they died will continue. Mankind is led into the darkness beyond our world by the inspiration of discovery and the longing to understand.

Our journey into space will go on.

In the skies today we saw destruction and tragedy. Yet farther than we can see, there is comfort and hope. In the words of the prophet Isaiah, "Lift your eyes and look to the heavens. Who created all these? He who brings out the starry hosts one by one and calls them each by name. Because of His great power, and mighty strength, not one of them is missing."

The same Creator who names the stars also knows the names of the seven souls we mourn today. The crew of the shuttle Columbia did not return safely to Earth; yet we can pray that all are safely home.

May God bless the grieving families. And may God continue to bless America.

15.4 Your Own Eulogy

For this activity, write your own eulogy. Questions to guide you include:

1. How do you want to be remembered?

2. How do you see yourself?

3. Who would you want to deliver your eulogy?

Name: _____ *Section:* _____ *Date:* _____

15.5 Toasting and Roasting

Your best friend is getting married. You are the maid of honor/best man. This means you have to give not one, but two speeches to honor your friend. The first of these will be at the bachelor/bachelorette party, where there is lots of room to "roast" your friend. The second speech will be given at the wedding reception, where you will focus on honoring your friendship, as well as the newly married couple's relationship. In the space provided below, list ways you will toast and roast your friend during these special events. How will the speeches be similar and/or different?

Bachelor/Bachelorette Party Roast

_____

_____

_____

_____

_____

Wedding Reception Toast

_____

_____

_____

_____

_____

15.6 Welcome to the Party

Think about an organization you are a part of. Write a "welcome" speech outline (full-sentence) for an event the organization holds annually. Remember to address the following questions in your speech/outline.

What is the exact purpose of the event? _____

_____

Who are the sponsors of the event? _____

_____

What are the history and goals of the sponsoring group? _____

_____

How are these goals similar to the goals of the audience? _____

_____

Is the event formal or informal? _____

_____

How will you create enthusiasm about the event in your speech? _____

_____

Name: _____ *Section:* _____ *Date:* _____

Test Yourself

Match these vocabulary terms with the descriptions that best define them.

1. _____ Welcoming Speech
2. _____ Introductory Speech
3. _____ Speech of Presentation
4. _____ Acceptance Speech
5. _____ Master of Ceremonies
6. _____ Inspirational Speech
7. _____ Commemorative Speech
8. _____ Special Occasion Speech

a. Giving out honors or awards

b. To entertain

c. Overseeing the speaking event

d. Greeting the audience of an occasion

e. Presenting the keynote speaker

f. Speech of celebration

g. Receiving honors or awards

h. Appeal to human emotion

chapter sixteen

Understanding the Copyright Law– At Least an Awareness of the Law

Chapter Outline

I. The Term Copyright

  A. Examples of Copyright Infringements

    1. Some people willingly admit to infringing upon copyright and are able to justify their violation.

    2. The second is guilty by association or coercion.

    3. The third is that you are unaware something is protected.

  B. The term copyright may seem straightforward.

II. A little history lesson helps us understand the context for our current copyright law.

  A. Written expression has been with mankind almost since the beginning of time.

    1. Archeologists discovered libraries dating back to the third millennium B.C. in the ancient Near East (Casson, 2001).

    2. By medieval times, the Catholic church restricted the reproduction of books.

    3. In the mid 1400s, Gutenberg changed the world when he invented the first working movable type printing press.

      a. This press enabled the printed word to be reproduced more easily, quickly, and the price of a publication started to drop, making printed material more affordable.

      b. The printing press allowed common people to enter the literary world and this threatened the elite's power and control they had over the common man.

      * Prior restraint is a government prohibition of printing specified material.

    4. In 1518, King Henry VIII issued printing privileges to the printers loyal to the crown.

    5. In 1710, the British Parliament passed the country's first copyright law, which gave rights to the authors instead of the printers.

      a. The law, "An Act for the Encouragement of Learning, by Vesting the Copies of Printed Books in the Authors or Purchasers of Such Copies, during the Time Therein Mentioned," was passed during Queen Anne's eight-year of rule and became known as the "Statute of Eight Anne."

b. The idea behind this law was to promote the creative mood and allow authors to financially benefit from their work. This was accomplished by giving ownership of literary property to the person who created the work or to the person the author gave ownership (Pember, 2000).

6. The "Statute of Eight Anne" was applied as law to Colonial America until the Revolutionary War when Article 1, Section 8 of the United States Constitution provided a foundation for our copyright law (Pember, 2000).

7. In 1790, Congress passed a copyright law which was similar to the "Statute of Eight Anne."

* The law gave authors, who were citizens of United States, the right to protect books, maps, and charts for twenty-eight years, two fourteen-year terms (Pember, 2000).

B. The copyright law does not work in isolation.

1. Prior restraint is a method for the government to control the message given to the people.

2. Almost all governments have practiced prior restraint at one time or another.

C. Copyright assumes originality.

D. Our copyright law tries to keep the spirit of the law and changes with technological advancements and as our definition of intellectual property expands.

1. In 1802, the copyright law included protection for print.

2. In 1831, the length of time for protection increased an additional fourteen years; musical compositions also gained protection.

3. In 1865, photographs were given protection.

4. Protection was provided for works of fine art and translations in 1870.

5. The copyright law underwent a major revision in 1909, which expanded the length of protection and attempted to balance public interest and the rights of the copyright owner (Pember, 2000 & Masciola, 2002).

6. The last major revision of the copyright law was in 1976.

a. This revision attempted to address technological developments, and to bring the United States into compliance with the international copyright laws as specified in the Berne Convention (Masciola, 2002).

b. The Berne Convention is an international copyright agreement enacted in 1887, and today is administered by the World Intellectual Property Organization (WIPO).

c. In 1989, the United States joined the Berne Convention (Bucy, 2002).

III. What exactly is copyright?

A. The concept of copyright deals with intangible and intellectual property–property you can't see or touch.

B. The copyright law specifies eight copyrightable categories.

1. Literary works;

2. Musical works, including any accompanying words;

3. Dramatic works, including any accompanying words;

4. Pantomimes and choreographic works;

5. Pictorial, graphic, and sculptural works;

6. Motion pictures and other audiovisual works;

7. Sound recordings; and,

8. Architectural works for a limited time.

C. These categories should be viewed broadly, because changing and new technology adds ways of creating original works almost daily.

IV. Exceptions to Copyright

A. The term "fair-use" allows some relaxation of the copyright law.

1. This exception intends to alleviate copyright restrictions to educators and researchers in some incidences so their work will not be stifled by the law and to encourage art and science.

2. Fair-use allows a certain amount of copying and distributing without the copyright owner's permission or compensation (Pember, 2000).

B. There are limitations to fair-use and is not the great loophole for unrestricted copying or distribution of copyrighted material in the name of education or self-use.

C. Fair-use is using copyrighted work for a legitimate purpose such as research, scholarship, criticism, news reporting, teaching, and the like.

* It is considered fair after examination of four open-ended set of factors: 1) the purpose and character of the use; 2) the nature of the work; 3) the amount used; and 4) the impact (actual or potential) on the market for, or value of, the work (Burke, 1993 & Burgunder, 2004).

D. The Fair-Use Doctrine has some flexibility with copyright restrictions, but fair-use does not have a set test or definition of what constitutes fair-use.

V. Owning the Copyright

A. The copyright law refers to the creator of original works as the copyright owner.

1. The creator is not always the copyright owner.

2. A concept under the copyright law that is not easily defined or understood. When ownership is in dispute, the courts decide.

B. Several alternatives attempt to clarify copyright ownership.

1. One alternative is a "shop right" amendment. This would allow the employee-author to be the legal author and copyright owner of works created within the scope of employment, and the employer would have the right to use the works for its own business purposes (Kilby, 1995).

2. Another option is to exempt "professional" employees from works made for hire.

C. Technology has hurt the copyright owner, and there is a need for stronger laws and greater enforcement. The other side says technology promotes new work with no financial lose, and might increase financial gain.

1. The Internet also poses major problems for copyright owners.

2. The No Electronic Theft (NET) Act is an amendment to Section 506 of the Copyright Act, and directly addresses Internet file sharing, including not for profit.

D. The new technologies and Internet fuel the opponents' argument that the copyright law is outdated because their existence makes it impossible to enforce the law.

1. These opponents also argue that copying and distributing copyrighted material does not affect sales, but instead pushes that product into the mainstream and increases sales (Bucy, 2002).

2. In the early days of the software revolution, software companies copy-protected their software, which prohibited the legal owner from making a backup copy, much less a copy for a friend.

E. Some people believe copyright is an outdated concept.

1. Proponents of the law argue there is a need for copyright protection.

2. If the author or creator was not guaranteed some type of legal protection anyone could take their original idea, copy it as their own idea, sell it, and get the financial and other benefits that rightly belong to the author or creator.

3. The argument continues that it wouldn't take long before the creative stopped creating because they aren't getting the benefit or reward for their work (Pember, 2000 & Zelezny, 2001).

VI. What is not protected by the law?

A. Not everything is eligible for copyright protection.

B. The law specifies four areas that are not protected by copyright law.

1. Works that have **not** been fixed in a tangible form of expression–for example, choreographic works that have not been notated or recorded, or improvisational speeches or performances that have not been written or recorded.

2. Titles, names, short phrases, and slogans; familiar symbols or designs; mere variations of typographic ornamentation, lettering, or coloring; mere listings of ingredients or contents.

3. Ideas, procedures, methods, systems, processes, concepts, principles, discoveries, or devices, as distinguished from a descriptive, explanation, or illustration.

4. Works consisting **entirely** of information that is common property and containing no original authorship–for example: standard calendars, height and weight charts, tape measures and rulers, and lists or tables taken from public documents or other common sources (United States Copyright Office, 2002).

C. Facts cannot be copyrighted.

1. The person who discovers a fact may not be able to claim ownership for that fact.

2. There is some protection for gathering the facts. This is known as "sweat of the brow" doctrine.

3. The idea behind this concept is if you spent time finding the facts and arranging them you should have some limited protection and reap the financial benefits (Pember, 2000).

D. News events also fall under noncopyrightable material.

VII. Obtaining a Copyright

A. The author automatically gains copyright and ownership when the work is created and fixed in a copy or phonorecord for the first time.

B. The copyright notice must be visually perceptible on copies and should contain three elements: (1) the symbol: © (the letter C in a circle), or the word "Copyright," or the abbreviation "Copr." (2) the year of first publication of the work, and (3) the name of the copyright owner.

C. Registration with the United States Copyright Office is separate from copyright and is not automatic.

1. The copyright holder must register the work with the United States Copyright Office.

2. Registration is not necessary for protection but gives the copyright owner more legal power if there is an infringement.

3. Registration is a legal formality which makes a public record of the copyright claim.

4. To register a copyright, the owner must send three elements in the same envelop or package to the Library of Congress, Copyright Office, 101 Independence Ave., SE, Washington, DC 20559-6000. The package must have a completed copy of the proper application form (available through the US Copyright Office), a nonrefundable filing fee, a nonreturnable copy of the work being registered (United States Copyright Office, 2002). Check with the US Copyright Office at <http://www.copyright.gov/> for the current filing fee and appropriate application form.

VIII. How long do copyrights last?

A. The length of copyright protection is one of those nuances in the law.

1. Depending on when the work was published or created depends on how long it is protected.

2. All work created (put in a tangible form) after January 1, 1978 is protected from the moment of creation for the lifetime of the author plus an additional 70 years. If there is more than one author, then protection is 70 years after the last surviving author's death (United States Copyright Office, 2002).

3. Protection for works made for hire and anonymous and pseudonymous works (unless the Copyright Office is given the identity of the author) is 95 years from publication or 120 years from creation whichever is shorter (United States Copyright Office, 2002).

4. If a work was created before January 1, 1978 but never published or registered with the Copyright Office, it is automatically brought under the same duration as works created after January 1, 1978 (United States Copyright Office, 2002).

5. Copyright protection for works originally created and published or registered before January 1, 1978 and under the Copyright Act of 1909 initially last for 28 years and may be renewed for an additional 28 years.

6. The copyright holder must renew the copyright to gain the additional 28 years. The 1976 Copyright Act extended the renewal term from 28 years to 47 years for a total of 75 years of protection (United States Copyright Office, 2002).

B. The terms of protection may not be as simple as when the work was created and if the copyright was registered.

C. Public domain is not an open and shut case.

IX. Plagiarism, Trademarks, and Patents

A. Plagiarism is passing off someone else's ideas, words, or thoughts as your own (Pember, 2000).

B. A trademark is used to identify a person or company's goods and services from the competition's products and services.

1. It is the trademark that tells the consumer you are getting the product you think you are purchasing.

2. Trademarks eliminate consumer confusion and clearly identify a product or service with a company (Pember, 2000).

3. Trademarks must be registered with the Patent and Trademark Office and then renewed five years later.

4. In 1996, Congress passed the Federal Dilution Trademark Act. This law gives trademark owners additional protection by giving them legal recourse if their trademark, or a similar trademark, is used on a dissimilar product.

C. Patent law is a federal statute, the Patent Act.

1. There are two types of patents, utility and design (Radcliffe, 2001).

2. Patent rights may only be claimed after the U.S. government issues the patent (Pember, 2000).

3. Utility patents apply to any new and useful process, machine, manufacture, or composition of matter, and they may be electrical, mechanical, or chemical.

4. A design patent is an ornamental design for articles of manufacture.

D. Obtaining a trademark or patent is not automatic and cannot be registered as easily or cheaply as copyright.

1. If you want a trademark or patent, you must hire a patent attorney and pay higher registration fees.

2. To take advantage of trademark or patent protection, you must have a valid registered trademark or patent.

Name: _____ Section: _____ Date: _____

16.1 Works Cited Practice Page

Correctly put the following titles in the correct format (MLA or APA) for a works cited page for a paper about sports.

James L. Shulman and William G. Bowen *College sports and educational values: the game of life.* Princeton University Press, Princeton New Jersey, 2001

William G. Bowen and Sarah A. Levin *Reclaiming the game: College sports and educational values.* Princeton University Press, Princeton New Jersey, 2003

The Meaning of Sports: Why Americans watch baseball, football, and basketball and what they see when they do. Michael Mandelbaum. PublicAffairs. New York, New York. 2004.

True Believers: The tragic inner life of sports fans. Joe Queenan. Picador. New York, New York. 2003.

Northeastern University Press. 2000. Boston, MA. Susan Birrell and Mary G. McDonald. *Reading sports: critical essays on power and representation.*

Bowman & Littlefield Publishers, Inc. Lanham, Maryalnd. 2003. *Fair and Foul: Beyond the Myths and Paradoxes of Sport.* 2nd Edition. D. Stanley Eitzen.

16.2 Outlines with Sources

Citing sources at the end of your outline is just as important as citing sources verbally in your speech. In the space provided, write synonyms for the two phrases: according to and reports . Then rewrite a paragraph of your speech; citing one of your sources, using one of the synonyms you came up with.

Paragraph with new citation and synonym

_____

_____

_____

_____

_____

_____

_____

_____

_____

_____

_____

Name: _____ *Section:* _____ *Date:* _____

16.3 Pay Attention to the Symbols

A copyright symbol is usually symbolized by a c in a circle (©). In your own words, explain why it is important to pay attention to the copyright symbol and why plagiarism is wrong.

_____

_____

_____

_____

_____

_____

_____

_____

_____

16.4 Music Copyrights

For the past several years there has been a debate about copying music for free. With the advent of Web sites where people could file-share, music swapping became easier and easier to do. Some artists are for file-swapping, saying it allows them to reach a wider audience, while other artists disagree, saying it is a copyright infringement, and it is affecting their record sales. What do you think?

_____

_____

_____

_____

_____

_____

_____

_____

_____

Name: _____ *Section:* _____ *Date:* _____

16.5 Categories of Copyright

As discussed in Chapter 16, there are eight categories protected under the copyright law. In the space provided, write down examples for each of the categories. Make sure that you provide proper citation for each example (APA or MLA format).

	Example One	Example Two
Literary Works		
Musical Works		
Dramatic Works		
Pantomimes and Choreographic Works		
Pictoral, Graphic, and Sculptural Works		
Motion Pictures and Other AV Works		
Sound Recordings		
Architectural Works		

16.6 Protecting Your Own Work

You've just written the best song, idea, or paper, and you want to make sure no one steals your idea. Visit the United States Copyright Office's website, at <http://www.copyright.gov/>, and write down the steps you will need to take to get your document registered.

1.

2.

3.

4.

5.

6.

7.

8.

9.

10.

Name: _____   *Section:* _____ *Date:* _____

Test Yourself

Match these vocabulary terms with the descriptions that best define them.

1. _____ Copyright Law

2. _____ Intangible/
   Intellectual Property

3. _____ Fair Use

4. _____ Plagiarism

5. _____ Trademark

6. _____ Utility Patents

7. _____ Design Patents

8. _____ Copyright Length

a. Relaxing of copyright law for research/education

b. Apply to new and useful processes and machines

c. Using other's ideas as your own

d. Usually 70 to 95 years

e. Apply to ornamental design

f. Protected by copyright

g. Used to identify ownership of goods

h. Prohibits duplication

Appendix A

Sample Speech Outlines

Special Occasion Speech Outline (Self-Introduction Speech)

I. Introduction

    A. I often find myself wondering how different my life would be if it weren't for the people in it.

    B. Today, I would like to tell you a little bit about my past, present, and future through sharing some of my most prized possessions.

Transition Statement: To start with, I would like to tell you a little about the bag my objects are in.

II. Body

    A. This backpack is important to me because I have had it since high school.

        1. I have gone on many travels using this bag to hold my belongings.

            a. I have taken it camping, to the beach, and to the mountains.

            b. The most exotic place this bag has traveled is Ireland.

        2. As you can see, the seams are beginning to fray from overuse, especially since I tended to overstuff it with books during graduate school.

Transition Statement: Now that I've told you about my bag, let me show you the item that represents my past.

    B. This stuffed animal I have also had since high school.

        1. He is named after a good friend of mine, named Brian.

        2. When I need some comfort or something to snuggle with, Brian-Bear is never very far away.

Transition Statement: The item I brought to represent my present was also a gift from a friend.

    C. This is my UCONN Huskies 2004 NCAA Basketball Men and Women's Championship t-shirt.

        1. This shirt was given to me by one of my friends for my birthday last year.

        2. It is important to me because the Huskies are my favorite NCAA basketball team, and I was very happy when they won the title.

Transition Statement: The t-shirt represents my present because I spend a lot of time watching basketball, but in the future I probably won't have that much time to do that.

    D. The final item in my bag, representing my future, is my wireless router card, also a birthday gift from a friend.

        1. Not only is wireless computing the "wave of the future," but it is important to my future too.

        2. As I move forward into my doctoral program, I can use my wireless router card to do research on my computer, virtually anywhere.

Transition Statement: Now that you have seen the items that represent me, I hope you have gained a better understanding of who I am, and what is important to me.

III. Conclusion

    A. You may have noticed that all of my objects were gifts given to me by my friends.

    B. I hope, as the future moves forward, I will continue to have the wonderful friendships that I have now, as well as to acquire new relationships along the way.

Informative Speech Outline

I. Introduction

   A. Attention-Getter: Narcissus, a Man from Greek Mythology.

      1. After spending countless hours admiring himself in the reflection of a stream, the gods retaliated and transformed the self-centered figure into a flower.

      2. While the gods once used the flower to crush egos, today the gods have reversed their call, producing a flower that gives some that little extra ego boost.

   B. Thesis

      1. As the *Dallas Morning News* of September 15, 1997 reports, it is "a medical breakthrough–one that could affect millions of people who suffer from mild depression."

      2. This unusual type of flower power is called St. John's Wort.

   C. Preview: We will first explore the history and folklore behind the flower. Next, we'll get an understanding of the applications or uses of St. John's Wort. And finally, we'll look at the advantages as well as the disadvantages of "nature's own Prozac."

Transition: Now with the way St. John's Wort has been making headlines and being featured on primetime news programs, you would think that the discovery of this flower power was made recently.

II. Body

   A. History of St. John's Wort

      1. St. John's Wort has been used for more than 2000 years.

        a. The *Buffalo News* of July 1, 1997 reports, "Father of Medicine–Hipprocrates used the orangey-yellow flowered plant to treat illnesses."

        b. In ancient Greece, it was used to chase away evil spirits.

        c. During the crusades, the flower was used to treat the wounds on the battlegrounds.

        d. Monks of the medieval time prescribed St. John's Wort for those afflicted with depression.

        e. In the Middle Ages, the flower was used for those who were considered insane and afflicted with melancholia.

        f. People in the Middle Ages, as found in an article in *the Kansas City Star*, slept with a sprig of the plant underneath their pillows on the eve of the holiday known as St. John's Tide. They thought that by doing this they would have the saint's protection against death in the following year.

      2. The origin of the name is almost as old.

        a. The July 28, 1997 *Kansas City Star* article has the yellow flower being named after John the Baptist by early Christians after his death.

        b. Another story has the name being derived from the Knights of St. John of Jerusalem who fought during the crusades.

        c. The legend of St. John's Wort is getting out.

B. Uses of St. John's Wort

   1. Although a vast majority of those taking St. John's Wort use it for helping them cope with mild depression, others find it has the ability to relieve female menstrual discomfort, to, even more recently, AIDS.

      a. The *Minneapolis Star Tribune* of September 14, 1997 reports, "researchers are currently investigating it (St. John's Wort) as an adjunct to other AIDS drugs that suppress HIV production."

      b. Experiments were done where HIV-infected mice were given St. John's Wort extract. The virus's progress was halted.

      c. The experiments were then taken one step further and human HIV and AIDS patients were given the extract from the flower.

      d. The results are inconclusive, though significant improvement was seen in some of the patients.

      e. Researchers have also launched clinical trails of St. John's Wort use in reducing fever and swelling of lymph nodes, and improving the immune system. For the millions of American afflicted with AIDS or HIV that is some awesome flower power.

   2. Some consider St. John's Wort has a healing ointment when applied to wounds.

      a. As the *Des Moines Register* of September 19, 1997 informs us, "Terry Condor said he recently stabbed himself accidentally with a screwdriver. As is his custom, he used topical herbs on the wound, but noticed it healed in three days–much sooner than he expected. He attributed that his success was to the use of hypericum–the Latin term for St. John's Wort."

   3. The flowering tops of St. John's Wort are prepared into an oil.

      a. This liquidly substance is then used for backaches or skin inflammations.

      b. The *Medical Economics Publishing Drug Topics* of September 1, 1997 reports, "The flowering tops are made into an oil or cream for topical treatment of burns and inflammations of the skin and muscles."

   4. St. John's Wort has gained attention through the recent developments in the weight loss pills controversy.

      a. Because of the recent FDA ban of two diet pills, those weight-loss seekers are turning to hypericum, an over-the-counter product made from St. John's Wort.

      b. The *New York Times* of September 18, 1997 reports, "The Food and Drug Administration has not approved use of St. John's Wort as an antidepressant since it is legally a dietary supplement."

C. Disadvantages

   1. The book *Hypericum and Depression* says only 2.4 percent of patients in one study had any side effects at all.

      a. These side effects include mild gastrointestinal discomfort, more commonly known as gas, usually relieved by taking the herb with big meals and a large of glass of water, fatigue, dry mouth, dizziness, skin rashes, and itching.

      b. Other side effects include allergic reactions, nausea, restlessness, tiredness, and vomiting.

      c. Some people experience an elevation of enzymes in the liver.

2. It is not for everybody.
    a. When St. John's is combined with other antidepressants such as Prozac, as an article in the September 14, 1997 *Minneapolis Star Tribune* reports, it can result in a serotonin overload, causing sweating, agitation, confusion and tremors.
    b. The *Raleigh News and Observer* of September 6, 1997 reports, "not for children under two or for pregnant or nursing women."
    c. Those who take St. John's Wort should be extremely careful when mixing the substance with tyramine, found in some foods like aged natural cheeses, cottage cheese, yogurt, caviar, and some wine.

III. Conclusion
    A. Review: By exploring this flower's past, it's current applications, and the mild side effects, we can now surely understand why the Gods reversed their call and produced "nature's own Prozac."
    B. Thesis: Nature's own Prozac is called St. John's Wort.
    C. Leave them wanting more: It enables thousands of users to feel a little bit better about themselves by raising the serotinin level in their body. For Amanda Lovato, the power of this flower has enabled her to gain weight, get her depression under control, and get better grades in school. Not every flower can do that.

Persuasive Speech Outline

I. Introduction

  A. Attention-Getter

    1. Last spring, Albert and Marianne Hassan were driving their mid-size Chrysler when they were side-swiped at an intersection, a scenario that usually only means damage to the car. But according to the October 5, 1997 *Sacramento Bee*, the side swiper was driving a Chevy Suburban. Its high front end pushed in the Hassan's driver side door, hitting Albert in the chest, killing him instantly. The Suburban then shoved the Chrysler sideways for fifty feet, crushing the passenger side against a tree. Mrs. Hassan was blinded and critically injured. The driver of the Suburban left the scene without a scratch.

    2. Unfortunately, scenes like this have become all too familiar, as routine accidents become tragic due to the destructive nature of sport utility vehicles. The "Big Three" automakers have made huge profits by telling us that sport utility vehicles can drive over mountains.

  B. Thesis

    1. What they've kept secret is that this design leads to devastating consequences for the rest of us on the road.

    2. The *Austin American Statesman* of September 28, 1997 reveals that accidents between a sport utility vehicle and a car kill more people than those involving two cars.

    3. This, despite the fact that for every six cars on the road, there is only one sport utility vehicle.

    4. Considering the miles most of us travel on a regular basis, this dangerous trend must be stopped.

  C. Preview: To understand why, let us first see why sport utility vehicles (SUVs) are so dangerous. Next, uncover why the hazards continue. And finally, suggest some realistic solutions, so an SUV won't leave us Dead On Arrival (DOA).

II. Body

  A. How Sport Utility Vehicles Are Dangerous.

    1. The September 11, 1997 episode of ABC's 20/20 reveals "the problems stems from the fact that these vehicles were initially designed for off-road use."

      a. For example, they sit higher off the ground and their suspensions are softer, allowing them to go over rougher terrain.

      b. Second, because most SUVs are designed with high ground clearance, the bumpers and frames of many SUVs are higher off the road than the bumpers of passenger cars.

      c. As the *Dallas Morning News* of March 30, 1997 suggests in the words of Robert Knoll, director of automobile testing for Consumer Reports magazine, "SUVs are generally ten inches higher than passenger cars. They tend to hit cars in structurally weak places. It many cases, it would go over the bumper and into parts of the vehicle that aren't designed to take the impact."

    2. Another danger found in SUVs are the way SUVs are built.

      a. As the *New York Times* of October 17, 1997 informs us, "Sport utility vehicles tend to have stiff frames that crumple the other vehicle in crashes."

      b. Moreover, Gerald Donaldson, senior research director at Advocates for Highway and Auto Safety, revealed in the previously cited *Dallas Morning*

News, "When the steel beams that form a SUVs rectangular underbody encounter the thinner steel lattice of an automobile's shell, they tend to inflict a lot of damage."

    c. Furthermore, the weight of SUVs is becoming a lot heavier, which is potentially more dangerous. The extra weight can make a bad crash worse. As the *New York Times* of September 24, 1997 reports, "Take a collision between a 2,900 pound Honda Accord and a 6,000 pound Chevrolet Suburban. The Accord driver would be at least 13 times as likely to be killed as the Suburban driver."

Transition Statement: One would think that with all these dangers something would have been done by now.

B. The hazards of SUVs are continuing for two big reasons: the "Big Three" automakers: Ford, General Motors, and Chrysler, and the government.

    1. It seems that the "Big Three" automakers have adopted the don't ask, don't tell policy.

        a. The *New York Times* of September 24, 1997 reports, "Automakers in the United States have paid little attention to the problem.

        b. Engineers at the auto makers say they work mainly on protecting the occupants of the vehicles they design and have no formal procedures for calculating and reducing the risk to occupants of other vehicles."

        c. Furthermore, they have ignored how the design of a vehicle may affect other vehicles in a crash, contending that it is the weight difference, and not design, that determines who lives and who dies in crashes.

        d. Moreover, automakers tend to focus more on air bags and other safety gear instead of demanding so-called compatible designs of passenger cars.

        e. Finally, Daniel F. Becker, of the Sierra club, states in the March 14, 1997 edition of the *New York Times*, that "people buy SUVs because they think they're safe. The Automakers actually believe they are giving the consumers what they want as they keep telling us, the consumers 'Big is safe.'"

C. The second reason the hazards of SUVs is continuing is because the federal government has been paying little attention to the hazards of SUVs.

    1. The *New York Times* of September 28, 1997 reveals, "Federal safety standards are still based on requiring to withstand collisions with other cars.

        a. U.S. regulators do not know what happens when a SUV hits a car. The federal money designated for an SUV car collisions study has been spent instead on air bag analyses for the last two years."

        b. Plus, the tests used to determine the safety of SUVs are inadequate. One such test is the pass-fail test. In order to be determined legal for sale, a SUV must crash into a barrier at 30 miles per hour without producing too much damage to two buckled dummies. But in Europe when an SUV is crashed into a passenger car at 40 miles per hour, the dummy is determined to be dead.

D. Now, with these dangers and with the current status quo in mind, what might be done to reduce the chances of dying from or in an SUV?

    1. First, as the *New York Times* of October 3, 1997 states, the "Big Three" automakers need to change the designs of their SUVs.

        a. As explained by the *Kansas City Star* of September 4, 1997, "less stiff frames could be less safe for the people in the trucks.

b. SUVs should be made with frames that bend more on impact, absorbing energy in a crash."

c. The *Asbury Press* of August 15, 1997 states, "Cutting a few pounds off heavy vehicles looks like a good way to achieve the goal" of safety.

d. Furthermore, the "Big Three" automakers should follow their German counterpart, Mercedes.

e. As the *New York Times* of September 24, 1997 reveals, "Mercedes-Benz has gone to great lengths to reduce the threat that SUVs possess in its new $34,445 sport utility vehicle. Below and behind the bumper is a hollow, horizontal tube that amounts to a second bumper at the same height as a car's underbody. The tube and two hollow steel boxes behind it are designed to crush during crashes, absorbing energy that might otherwise be transmitted to either vehicle's occupants. Mercedes crashed the vehicle at 31 miles per hours into a Mercedes so small it is not sold in the United States; a crash dummy in the car 'survived.'"

2. Second, the federal government should require the Automakers to design better crash tests, similar to those already conducted in Europe.

a. The government should run the tests and publish the results, encouraging the consumers to shop for safety.

b. The federal government should direct insurance companies to increase premiums for liability coverage on sport utility vehicles. Now policyholders pay roughly the same premium for liability protection whether they owned an ordinary sedan or two-ton pickup. But, as revealed in the October 27, 1997 issue of *Time* magazine, "Farmers Insurance Group, the nation's third largest insurer, has already lifted premiums as much as ten percent." Similar plans should be developed at other insurance companies. As a result, owners of SUVs may see their insurance bills jump on the liability coverage.

c. Finally, the government should require all vehicles to have bumpers of the same height, and steel beams in SUVs frames with lighter, steel-lattice, unibody designs should be replaced.

3. This is what we, as consumers, can do.

a. First, when purchasing a SUV, ask for results from crash study tests. Don't buy a vehicle on looks or whether the stereo system is good or not. Don't buy an SUV believing "Bigger is safer."

b. Second, research to find out if your SUV is unsafe. You can do this by visiting www.nhsta.dot.gov.

c. Third, share your knowledge with a friend, coworker, or even family member about what you know about the dangers of SUVs.

d. And finally, look out for SUVs on the road. Be aware. Be alert.

Transition Statement: What happened to Albert and Marianne Hassan last spring was tragic.

III. Conclusion

A. Tie-in to an attention getter: Their three-year-old son, who was waiting for them across town, will now grow up without his father. His mother will never be able to see him start kindergarten, play little league, or even get married, all because a vehicle that was bigger and heavier than their passenger car hit them.

B. Review of preview and thesis: Knowing the hazards of SUVs, why these hazards are continuing, and finally suggesting some realistic solutions, we now know what we can do to prevent an SUV from leaving us DOA.

Appendix B

Sample Speech and Essay Rubrics

Special Occasion Speech Evaluation Form

Evaluation

Speeches will be constructively evaluated on vocal quality, posture, absence of verbal fillers, organization of presentation, eye contact, and the originality and depth of your discussion of your name. The evaluation of this assignment will be essential to the success of subsequent presentations. *The grade assigned will reflect perceived effort in relation to the evaluation criteria.*

<u>E</u>xcellent (10)   <u>A</u>bove Average (8)   <u>S</u>atisfactory (6)   <u>N</u>eeds Improvement (4)

Presentation:

Organized Well	E	A	S	N
Edited Well	E	A	S	N
Stayed Within Time Limit	E	A	S	N
Sustained Eye Contact	E	A	S	N
Confident, Relaxed Posture	E	A	S	N
Conversational Quality	E	A	S	N
Adequate Volume	E	A	S	N
Fluency, Well Rehearsed	E	A	S	N
Absence of Verbal Fillers	E	A	S	N
Enthusiastic Presentation	E	A	S	N

Grade: _____

Additional Comments:

Group Project Evaluation Form

Paper Content

Step by step (using the problem-solving procedure), you are to analyze and solve the problem. As a group you are to turn in a five-page analysis of the problem-solving process that took place within your group. Your paper should include a minimum of three references. References should not be more than five years old. Cite using APA format. In your paper, you are to discuss:

1. The best alternative and explain why and how your group came to this conclusion. (3.5-5 pages) [15 pts]	
2. Challenges your group faced. (.5 pages) [4 pts]	
3. Conflicts that arose. (.5 pages) [4 pts]	
4. Successes. (.5 pages) [4 pts]	
5. Transcript of all online discussions (Should meet online at least twice) [4 pts]	

Paper Content Total (31)

Problem-Solving Procedure Content

1. Define the problem (7)	
2. Research and analyze the problem (7)	
3. Establish a checklist of criteria (7)	
4. List possible alternatives (7)	
5. Evaluate each alternative (7)	
6. Select the best alternative (7)	
7. Group conflicts and challenges (7)	
8. Group successes (7)	
Problem-Solving Procedure Content Total (56)	
Grammar (6)	
APA Format (7)	
Group Project Grade (100)	

Informative/Persuasive Speech Evaluation Form

Evaluation

Appropriate topic choice, narrowed for the time limit.

Organization: Clear specific purpose and thesis, complete introduction, and conclusion, effective use of transitions, clear pattern, clear main points.

Content: Support adapted to knowledge and interest level of audience, sources cited.

Visual Aids: Prepared and presented well.

Delivery: Voice, eye contact, posture, gestures, dress, fluency, language use.

	Excellent	Satisfactory	Needs Improvement
Outline	E	S	N
Met Time Requirement	E	S	N
Introduction	E	S	N
Attention-getting material			
Thesis statement			
Body of Presentation	E	S	N
Clear organizational pattern			
Main points clear and elaborated			
Evidence Cited	E	S	N
All sources cited in speech			
All evidence cited in speech			
Credible/relevant evidence			
Verbal Presentation and Language	E	S	N
Rate			
Pitch			
Tone			
Volume			

Appropriate to audience and occasion

No slang

Pronunciation, grammar and articulation

Absence of verbal fillers

Nonverbal Presentation   E   S   N

Eye contact

Gestures

Not reading from note cards

Conclusion   E   S   N

Summary of argument

Final statement

Speech Grade: _____

Additional Comments:

Essay Evaluation Form

Evaluation

All essays are evaluated for content, clarity, and grammar. The following is a general break down of the grading scale for all essays.

A (100-90) – No grammar or spelling mistakes; essay contains introduction and conclusion; contained transitions between thoughts; directions were followed; meets length requirement; answered questions and provided "meat" to responses.

B (89-80) – Very few spelling or grammar mistakes (3 or 4); essays contains introduction and conclusion; directions were followed; meets length requirement; answered questions but only provided some "meat."

C (79-70) – Many grammar and spelling mistakes (more than 5); had only introduction or conclusion; flow of essay was choppy; answered questions with minimal "meat"; did not meet length requirements; turned in hand-written copy instead of typed.

D (69-60) – Too many grammar and spelling mistakes (more than 10); no introduction or conclusion; provided minimum responses to questions; did not meet length requirements.

F (59-0) – Did not follow directions to assignment; incomplete sentences and way too many grammar and spelling mistakes (over 20); essay lacked flow; did not meet length requirement; did not turn paper in on due date.

Appendix C

Test Yourself Answers

Chapter 1

1. I	2. D
3. H	4. F
5. C	6. J
7. B	8. E
9. G	10. A

Chapter 2

1. D	2. H
3. F	4. A
5. E	6. I
7. J	8. B
9. G	10. C

Chapter 3

1. D	2. H
3. J	4. F
5. A	6. E
7. C	8. G
9. B	10. I

Chapter 4

1. E	2. H
3. CD	4. A
5. F	6. G
7. D	8. B

Chapter 5

1. E	2. B
3. I	4. G
5. D	6. J
7. C	8. F
9. H	10. A

Chapter 6

1. D	2. H
3. G	4. C
5. J	6. F
7. B	8. I
9. E	10. A

Chapter 7

1. G	2. C
3. I	4. J
5. H	6. A
7. E	8. B
9. D	10. F

Chapter 8

1. E	2. G
3. D	4. J
5. A	6. I
7. B	8. F
9. H	10. C

Chapter 9

1. F	2. C
3. H	4. B
5. G	6. I
7. E	8. A
9. D	

Chapter 10

1. F	2. B
3. I	4. E
5. A	6. J
7. C	8. H
9. G	10. D

Chapter 11

1. F	2. E
3. H	4. A
5. G	6. C
7. D	8. B

Chapter 12

1. F	2. C
3. A	4. H
5. D	6. B
7. E	8. G

Chapter 13

1. G	2. D
3. J	4. A
5. H	6. E
7. B	8. I
9. F	10. C

Chapter 14

1. E	2. I
3. G	4. A
5. B	6. H
7. J	8. C
9. D	10. F

Chapter 15

1. D	2. E
3. A	4. G
5. C	6. H
7. F	8. B

Chapter 16

1. H	2. F
3. A	4. C
5. G	6. B
7. E	8. D